Expert Searching in the Google Age

Medical Library Association Books

The Medical Library Association (MLA) features books that showcase the expertise of health sciences librarians for other librarians and professionals.

MLA Books are excellent resources for librarians in hospitals, medical research practice, and other settings. These volumes will provide health care professionals and patients with accurate information that can improve outcomes and save lives.

Each book in the series has been overseen editorially since conception by the Medical Library Association Books Panel, composed of MLA members with expertise spanning the breadth of health sciences librarianship.

Medical Library Association Books Panel

Lauren M. Young, AHIP, chair
Kristen L. Young, AHIP, chair designate
Michel C. Atlas
Dorothy C. Ogdon, AHIP
Karen McElfresh, AHIP
Megan Curran Rosenbloom
Tracy Shields, AHIP
JoLinda L. Thompson, AHIP
Heidi Heilemann, AHIP, board liaison

About the Medical Library Association

Founded in 1898, MLA is a 501(c)(3) nonprofit, educational organization of 3,500 individual and institutional members in the health sciences information field that provides lifelong educational opportunities, supports a knowledgebase of health information research, and works with a global network of partners to promote the importance of quality information for improved health to the health care community and the public.

Books in the Series

The Medical Library Association Guide to Providing Consumer and Patient Health Information edited by Michele Spatz
Health Sciences Librarianship edited by M. Sandra Wood
Curriculum-Based Library Instruction: From Cultivating Faculty Relationships to Assessment edited by Amy Blevins and Megan Inman
Mobile Technologies for Every Library by Ann Whitney Gleason

Marketing for Special and Academic Libraries: A Planning and Best Practices Sourcebook by Patricia Higginbottom and Valerie Gordon

Translating Expertise: The Librarian's Role in Translational Research edited by Marisa L. Conte

Expert Searching in the Google Age by Terry Ann Jankowski

Expert Searching in the Google Age

Terry Ann Jankowski

ROWMAN & LITTLEFIELD
Lanham • Boulder • New York • London

Published by Rowman & Littlefield
A wholly owned subsidary of The Rowman & Littlefield Publishing Group, Inc.
4501 Forbes Boulevard, Suite 200, Lanham, Maryland 20706
www.rowman.com

Unit A, Whitacre Mews, 26-34 Stannary Street, London SE11 4AB

British Library Cataloguing in Publication Information Available

Library of Congress Cataloging-in-Publication Data

Names: Jankowski, Terry Ann, 1951– author. | Medical Library Association, issuing body.
Title: Expert searching in the Google Age / Terry Ann Jankowski.
Other titles: Medical Library Association books.
Description: Lanham : Rowman & Littlefield, [2016] | Series: Medical Library Association books | Includes bibliographical references and index.
Identifiers: LCCN 2016014439 (print) | LCCN 2016032163 (ebook) | ISBN 9781442239647 (cloth : alk. paper) | ISBN 9781442239654 (pbk. : alk. paper) | ISBN 9781442239661 (electronic)
Subjects: | MESH: Information Storage and Retrieval—methods | Medicine | Internet | Databases as Topic | Professional Role
Classification: LCC R858 (print) | LCC R858 (ebook) | NLM W 26.55.I4 | DDC 610.285—dc23 LC record available at https://lccn.loc.gov/2016014439

♾ ™ The paper used in this publication meets the minimum requirements of American National Standard for Information Sciences Permanence of Paper for Printed Library Materials, ANSI/NISO Z39.48-1992.

Printed in the United States of America

Contents

Preface

Librarians, especially reference librarians, have always been expert searchers. What else is sifting through the mountains of print representations of human knowledge to answer questions posed to us but searching through an enormous database? Having it digitized and at our fingertips has made it quicker, and for the most part easier. At the same time, it presents its own set of challenges and complexities.

As the web has evolved and better search engines developed, librarians have become more accustomed to our customers using Google, Bing, or Wikipedia as their first,[1, 2] if not last, stop in searching; many of us have learned to use the web as a jumping-off point ourselves. As users struggle to find information, librarians have gained greater recognition for their searching skills in addition to an acknowledgment of the benefits they bring to the table in the educational, clinical, and research arenas.[3] Performing systematic reviews for evidence-based medicine has become standard practice and librarians are called upon to support them. Both researchers and librarians are still hungry for information on how to create these complex searches. Additionally, librarians continue to seek out ideas for proving their worth as well as establishing and marketing search services. Faculty interviewed as part of the Ethnographic Research in Illinois Academic Libraries (ERIAL) Project declared that students were weak in finding and evaluating research tools beyond Google and Wikipedia, critically appraising evidence, and narrowing the research focus.[4] Instructors also felt this was an area in which librarians could help. This book, *Expert Searching in the Google Age*, examines many of these complexities and offers ideas for ways of supporting both ourselves and others in searching for information.

Although the primary target audience for this book is librarians, information specialists, and library school students in the health sciences, all with less than five years of experience routinely searching bibliographic databases, any potential searcher can benefit from the contents. Interviewing clients, analyzing databases, constructing and evaluating strategies, and managing information and services are universal skills. Most of the examples and databases described in the book concentrate on health and biomedical sciences (because those are my areas of expertise) but these techniques are transferable to any discipline.

HOW TO USE THIS BOOK

In the early days of mediated (i.e., expert, by librarians) searching, Barbara Quint identified seven stages of online searching (reference interview, tactical overview, database selection, search strategy formulation, the online search, feedback or reviewing results, and presenting final search results).[5] In today's more streamlined world, Maggio, Tannery, and Kanter have reduced the process to five steps: choose a database, select search terms, use Boolean operators to combine search terms, limit results, and explain the search process.[6] In this book, I chose to cover determining the search question, selecting and evaluating the resources, developing the search strategy, reviewing and evaluating the search, and documenting and managing the results, plus provide some additional information on librarians' roles, directions for searching, and useful tools.

Chapter 1 explores the evolution of expert searchers and sets the stage for the rest of the book. What do you and they *really* need to know before the search takes place? That is the topic covered by chapter 2 on search negotiation. Chapter 3 explores the issues around database selection and evaluation: What resources are available? What is the role of grey literature? How do you evaluate databases? This chapter also looks at database infrastructure and how searchers can use it and the interface to more efficiently find references. Chapter 4 builds on the information from chapters 2 and 3 to develop the actual search strategy, focusing on identifying the concepts in a search, using the best vocabulary for these concepts, and combining them for optimal search results. Examining search results and developing ways to refine and improve searches is covered in chapter 5, which also looks at using filters or protocols for better retrieval. Chapter 6 presents different ways of documenting and managing search results. Chapter 7 discusses some of the various search services librarians can and do offer. It also peeks into the future of searching. What's next on the horizon for database searching? Chapter 8 describes some tools and resources to help the expert searchers. The appendixes provide access to two key documents defining the roles and value of expert searchers. Exercises and examples (taken from either my own experiences or those of my colleagues) distributed throughout the text offer opportunities for application and practice. It may also be helpful to keep in mind a specific situation you are facing while reading the book and apply information gained as you go.

After completing the book, readers will have developed a better understanding of expert searching: what it is, its skills, and its impact on their professional lives. They also will have a set of checklists, skills, and tools they can use to negotiate, create, complete, and deliver searches. Although I recommend working through the book from start to finish, another approach is to consult specific chapters of interest. Or consider the following scenario as you read through the book to better understand and apply the concepts:

> As you scan your email, you see a request from a veterinarian. He tells you he is working with a sponsor who is willing to place animals in nursing homes. He shares that he is aware of some of the problems with pets (e.g., zoonoses transmitted), and has heard anecdotes about the benefits of pets for the elderly (e.g., improved moods and less illness). He has also heard about aquariums used with patients who have Alzheimer's disease and in dental offices for their calming effects. Can you find some studies showing a connection between the elderly and animals, especially regarding improvement of the immune system? Also, are there regulations and laws the veterinarian needs to be aware of? In short, what's the evidence that supports giving a senior citizen a pet? And what might be the drawbacks?
>
> What additional questions do you need to ask? Which databases would have relevant information? What search terms might you use?

NOTES

1. Duke, Lynda M, and Andrew D Asher, eds. *College Libraries and Student Culture: What We Now Know.* Chicago: ALA Editions, 2012: 34.

2. Head, Alison J. *Staying Smart: How Today's Graduates Continue to Learn Once They Complete College.* Project Information Literacy Research Report, January 5, 2016. http://projectinfolit.org/images/pdfs/2016_lifelonglearning_fullreport.pdf.

3. Sollenberger, Julia F, and Robert G Holloway Jr. "The Evolving Role and Value of Libraries and Librarians in Health Care," *JAMA* 310 (2013): 1231–1232.

4. Duke, Lynda M, and Andrew D Asher, eds. *College Libraries and Student Culture: What We Now Know.* Chicago: ALA Editions, 2012: 71.

5. Quint, Barbara. "Inside a Searcher's Mind: The Seven Stages of an Online Search," Part 1: "On-line Bibliographic Searching," *Online* 15 (1991): 13–18.

6. Maggio, Lauren A, Nancy H Tannery, and Steven L Kanter. "AM Last Page: How to Perform an Effective Database Search," *Academic Medicine* 86 (2013): 1057.

Chapter One

Evolution of Expert Searching

Before discussing the evolution of expert searching as well as librarians' roles and contributions to the search process, some definitions and background information may prove useful. End-user searching is commonly defined as database searching carried out by the person who will use the search results. It may be as simple as a quick search on the web for restaurant reviews or as complex as creating a set of documents to review for a research project. End-user searching occurs when the searcher is the one who will review, analyze, and utilize the information retrieved. Mediated searching, then, is when someone other than the end user does the search. The searcher is often referred to as an intermediary or expert. The terms "search specialist," "search analyst," "information professional," and "information specialist" have been used interchangeably to describe expert searchers.

The Medical Library Association (MLA) defines expert searching as "a mediated process in which a user with an information need seeks consultation and assistance from a recognized expert."[1] The experts team up with researchers, clinicians, and others to develop and run a well-defined literature search for evidence to support the learning, research, diagnostic, or treatment processes. These trained information specialists use their knowledge of database subject content and structure, indexing conventions, and information organization to efficiently retrieve and present results, thus bringing value to the search process by freeing the requester to focus on the problem at hand. Expert searchers can be found in a variety of settings (hospitals, laboratories, businesses, colleges, and all types of libraries): any place where their skills can be used to find information to assist in learning about or supporting such activities as development of accountable care networks, challenging clinical cases, patient education and safety, term papers, business and academic decisions, grant applications, and research design. Corporate librarians in particular fall into the category of expert searchers. Often their clients do not have ready access to databases and rely on their librarians to search for as well as manage their results.

EVOLUTION OF EXPERT SEARCHING

In the late 1960s as the first bibliographic databases and search systems were developed, database searching was always mediated by librarians or information specialists. These early expert searchers received weeks of training and frequently refreshed their skills by attending regular updates provided by database vendors, producers, and fellow librarians. Topics covered included database structure, vocabulary terms, database contents, and interface capabilities as well as interview and search construction techniques. Database construction and search courses were added to library school curriculums and an entire industry evolved around journals and conferences devoted to expert searching.

Searches were conducted while connected by a telephone line to the database and charged by the time they took to run and the number of references retrieved. Thinking through the search, identifying concepts and search terms, and drafting different approaches to the search and employing various shortcuts enabled searchers to make the most effective use of the online time. As a result of this preparation, expert searchers developed strong research skills and habits as well as a comprehensive knowledge of the databases used on a daily basis to help them become thoughtful and thorough database searchers.

Self-searching gradually became standard practice as individuals gained access to the web and personal computers. Database producers and vendors built more sophisticated and user-friendly interfaces so that less training was required to use them. This trend was led by the introduction of Grateful Med, an end-user interface for searching MEDLINE, by the National Library of Medicine (NLM) in 1986, quickly followed by user-friendly interfaces for databases from other producers. Vendors switched to access via the web and flat-rate licensing or subscriptions, reducing the need for extensive preparation before hopping on and searching. Just "Googling it" became the first, and often last, step in searching. Database producers took advantage of this approach and embarked on the quest to perfect the single search box. Librarians acquired new roles as consultants and trainers, although many still offered database search services for those who would rather spend their time using the search results than looking for references.

The untimely death of a volunteer participating in a clinical study in 2001 triggered a debate about and resurgence of interest in database searching by experts. Questions about who should search (i.e., end user or intermediary) and what constitutes a complete search were raised. Expert searchers reexamined their skills and asked themselves what they could bring to the table.

MLA responded by appointing a Taskforce on Expert Searching that produced a policy statement on the role of expert searching in health sciences libraries. MLA's statement provides a definition of expert searching, outlines the roles for librarians, and describes key areas in healthcare that can benefit by using librarians as expert searchers. (See appendix A for the complete text of the policy statement.) Librarians rallied around this call to action. A teleconference and a themed issue of MLA's journal appeared soon after the task force completed its work. Both an expert searching listserv and a recurring column in MLA's newsletter were established. A few years later, the Institute of Medicine reinforced the value of expert searchers by publishing guidelines that require consultation or utilization of search experts in searching the literature for writing systematic reviews. (See appendix B for the summary.) The frequency of workshops on and guidelines for creating and supporting systematic reviews increased exponentially. And additional groups of librarians formed discussion and research groups to support each other in expert searching. Today expert searchers are enjoying a renaissance of recognition. [2, 3]

ROLES FOR LIBRARIANS

An important professional role for librarians is that of expert searcher. Expert searchers can assume either the starring role in database searching (i.e., perform the search in its entirety) or a supporting role, such as coaching someone through the search process. In both roles, librarians bring added value to the search process with their skills and knowledge. Additional roles include the development of services and more comprehensive education for end users.

"Preliminary searches conducted by a librarian can help refine the question and determine its feasibility and scope." [4] Additionally, these authors and others [5] recognize that librarians are more familiar with the search process and intricacies of searching multiple databases to retrieve as much of the literature on a topic as possible. Although these statements referred to supporting physicians, the research process in any field can be improved by the participation of librarians. Librarians are trained in the search process described by Jerome and Jankowski [6] to interview and clarify the question, identify appropriate resources to search, create a strategy, search the database, and then evaluate and explain results, repeating the different steps as needed until the desired results are attained. By utilizing librarians to conduct the more complex searches, researchers can spend their time digesting and analyzing the literature.

For those who do want to perform their own searches, librarians take on the role of coach or educator. If the individual consultations at my institution are any indicator, more than 60% of them are teaching people how to build searchable questions as well as the intricacies of controlled vocabularies, contents of available databases, and search mechanics for different databases. As individuals come to rely more on search engines and discovery tools instead of specific databases, this role continues to evolve.

ATTRIBUTES AND SKILLS OF SEARCHERS

When describing college student searching behavior, Duke and Asher stated that "successful students must not only familiarize themselves with a discipline and its particular jargon but also must have an adequate understanding of how information is organized, how to evaluate sources, and how to use the 'tools' of scholarship, such as online catalogs [and] databases."[7] These are the very skills required by expert searchers.

When developing its competencies for information professionals of the 21st century,[8] the Special Library Association (SLA) explicitly stated that an information professional "applies expertise in databases, indexing, metadata, and information analysis and synthesis to improve information retrieval and use in the organization" and "demonstrates expert knowledge of the content and format of information resources, including the ability to critically evaluate, select and filter them." SLA's applied scenarios in the same document further describe how these abilities come into play while providing help with information resources and, by extrapolation, database searching. Note that this document is undergoing revision; I fully expect these abilities for database searching to remain.

MLA's policy statement on the role of expert searching also describes the many skills and attributes needed by an expert searcher, including communication skills, subject knowledge, self-recognition of his or her own abilities and knowledge, database knowledge (of its structure, content, and interface), and the use of reasoning, evaluation methods, and documentation skills. Are these inherent or can they be taught? Although anyone can learn the mechanics and techniques of searching, expert searchers require traits or abilities such as curiosity, tenacity, and problem solving to be successful. Many of the other skills, such as communication and evaluation methods, can be developed over time with practice and instruction. As a result, the "nature versus nurture" argument around expert searching will continue to be debated for years to come.

NOTES

1. Medical Library Association. "Role of Expert Searching in Health Sciences Libraries. Policy Statement by the Medical Library Association. Adopted September 2003," *Journal of the Medical Library Association* 93 (2005): 42–44.

2. Tan, Maria C, and Lauren A Maggio. "Expert Searcher, Teacher, Content Manager, and Patient Advocate: An Exploratory Study of Clinical Librarian Roles," *Journal of the Medical Library Association* 101 (2013): 63–72.

3. Perrier, Laure, Ann Farrell, A Patricia Ayala, David Lightfoot, Tim Kenny, Ellen Aaronson, Nancy Allee, Tara Brigham, Elizabeth Connor, Teodora Constantinescu, Joanne Muellenbach, Helen-Ann Brown Epstein, and Ardis Weiss. "Effects of Librarian-Provided Services in Healthcare Settings: A Systematic Review," *Journal of the American Informatics Association* 21 (2014): 118–124. doi: 10.1136/amiajnl-2014-002825.

4. Rethlefsen, Melissa L, M Hassan Murad, and Edward H Livingston. "Engaging Medical Librarians to Improve the Quality of Review Articles," *JAMA* 312 (2014): 999.

5. Sandieson, Robert W, Lori C Kirkpatrick, Rachel M Sandieson, and Walter Zimmerman. "Harnessing the Power of Education Research Databases with the Pearl-Harvesting Methodological Framework for Information Retrieval," *Journal of Special Education* 44 (2010): 161–175. doi: 10.1177/0022466909349144.

6. Jerome, Rebecca, and Terry Ann Jankowski. "Exploring the Components of the Expert Search," *MLA News* 362 (2004): 1.

7. Duke, Lynda M, and Andrew D Asher, eds. *College Libraries and Student Culture: What We Now Know.* Chicago: ALA Editions, 2012: 71.

8. Special Libraries Association. *Competencies for Information Professionals of the 21st Century.* Revised ed. Special Libraries Association, 2003. Available at http://sla.org/wp-content/uploads/2013/01/0_LRNCompetencies2003_revised.pdf.

Chapter Two

Search Question Definition and Negotiation

"An interview is a special kind of conversation."[1] Its primary purpose is to find out what the client *really* wants. Secondary objectives include establishing rapport, gathering background, setting expectations, and education. In order to discover the real question, you must allot sufficient time to listen more than talk and use open-ended questions to engage the requester. Asking questions becomes a sign of strength, not uncertainty; an acknowledgment of the requester's expertise and your desire to acquire more knowledge, leading to the formation of a strong partnership to develop and execute a successful search.

Negotiating the search parameters through a series of discussions or question-and-answer sessions (i.e., the reference interview) enables your client to clearly define his or her information needs. Requesters can indicate the depth and breadth of the topic as well as the extent and limits of their knowledge about the search subject or process. As the client talks through the question, he or she clarifies it for both of you and helps shape it into an answerable question. The explanations and answers given provide you with ideas for constructing a search strategy and selecting appropriate resources to use. Discussing such details as database selection, relevant search terms, the amount of information available on the topic, the size of the expected retrieval, and the length of the search process allows clients to develop realistic expectations about their specific search and database searching in general.

THE ART OF INTERVIEWING

Much has been written on the art of interviewing and negotiation. Key points to remember include being approachable, developing a sense of teamwork, achieving mutual understanding of the question, and establishing the boundaries of the search and search process. In this way, open communication can be established so that both of your needs are met. Some useful questions or phrases to accomplish these goals might include the following:

- Is now a good time to discuss your request or shall we schedule another time?
- Where would you like to meet?

These types of questions acknowledge the value of the client's time and provide for confidentiality of the interview. They also ensure that sufficient time is set aside to develop the question.

- Tell me more about the project.
- What's the current thinking on this subject?

Statements and questions such as these open the dialog to let the researcher share information or teach you where there might be gaps in your own knowledge that you will want to fill in prior to running the search without decreasing his confidence in your abilities. They also provide an opportunity for the requester to identify the real question, provide useful background, and clarify terminology.

- So you are interested in childhood obesity? Are there specific aspects of interest? Environmental factors, for example?
- How much information are you expecting? If there is more than that, should I look for specific types of articles or keywords in the title?

Paraphrasing the request back to the user allows you to check your understanding of the subject and question being asked as well as to establish parameters for the search. It also provides you with an opportunity to create more realistic expectations for the search (e.g., inform the requester that there may be more information than expected and suggest a way of limiting it to a useful amount).

- Have you seen any articles on this topic? Do you have those references?
- Where have you already looked?

Asking for this type of information allows you to gauge the depth of the researcher's knowledge of the topic and the existing literature as well as to identify the current terminology in the field. Additionally, you may receive a citation to a useful article that can either serve as the starting point for the search (a source of possible keywords or indexing terms) or an evaluation tool for the success of the search (if the article appears in the retrieval, the search can be judged successful) or educate you on the topic.

THE NEGOTIATION CYCLE

Like the research process, search negotiation passes through different stages, which may be repeated as needed: a pre-search interview, mid-search check-ins, and a post-search debriefing or evaluation upon completion. As results are obtained at the different stages and evaluated, the question may be judged complete, modified, or taken in another direction entirely.

The pre-search interview sets the stage for the process by focusing on the details of the search, educating the requester about the search process, and setting expectations for the journey and its outcome. Check-ins or mini-interviews during the search process further clarify the question and ensure that the search is moving in the desired direction. Post-search discussions provide additional opportunities for feedback and more information about the process or search results. Throughout the experience, trust and rapport are established so that you and the requester work together as a team to achieve the desired results. Sometimes the outcome may be that you coach the end user as he performs his own search: another application of expert searching skills. The goodwill generated by a successful search negotiation and results serves as an excellent marketing tool.

PRE-SEARCH INTERVIEW

The majority of the search negotiation occurs during the pre-search interview. In this stage, the interviewer determines what the requester *really* wants, both in terms of the results and the process. During this interaction, you establish rapport with the requester, clarify and negotiate the question, begin the identification of search terms, learn the context for the request, and establish working arrangements and expectations for the search as well as manage the minutiae of the search (e.g., collecting an email address for delivery of results). As the request is negotiated, you share the confidential nature of the process and reassure the client that questions asked are not meant to pry or annoy but rather to gather facts and relevant background to provide a useful end result. Throughout the interview, good communication must be established so that the desired results can be achieved together.

Occasionally, individuals are unable to work together. If this is the case, you should refer the question to another searcher if possible. Alternatively, the requester can designate someone else on his or her team to act as the negotiator with the librarian.

Working with a Third-Party Request

Other circumstances may also place you in the position of working with an intermediary. Frequently, a secretary, family member, research assistant, or single representative from a group project appears with the request. In these cases, the individual may know only some of the information about the topic or may be unclear about other parameters. The search negotiation drags on, with everyone becoming frustrated by the frequent stops and starts along the journey. One option to improve negotiation with a third party is to send a list of specific questions with the intermediary to the end user.

- Should the topic be restricted to human studies only?
- Are there some key authors or articles I should look for?
- Where have you already looked?

Of course, several rounds of this may be needed if only partial answers are returned or as other avenues are explored as the search progresses. As soon as more than one round has begun, it might be time to schedule a telephone or chat session with the entire group, especially if screen sharing or conferencing technologies are readily available. The latter method is made even more successful if you can flex your schedule to theirs, perhaps working outside of normal business hours. Whichever method is utilized, being respectful of the researchers' time by providing questions in advance and informing them of the length of the interview will improve relations—all part of developing good rapport.

If the additional details needed cannot be obtained, a search taken "as is" can still be attempted. A note or formal cover letter included with the results should include a copy of the search strategy, list any concerns about the results, and offer to rerun the search as needed. Often, when given search results that don't match their expectations, requesters will return for more information if the offer has been made in advance.

Interview Checklist

Surgeons and pilots use checklists to prevent errors,[2] especially errors of omission. Given the multiple objectives of a reference interview, using a checklist will also help you achieve a successful search by ensuring that all the relevant questions are asked. Although it may appear that experienced librarians conduct reference interviews off the cuff, most of them have in their heads a predetermined list of questions to ask. Using a printed or electronic form also provides you with notes to use when building the search strategy. And finally, because searches so often provide the evidence to build a guideline or make a decision, the notes can be used to document the search for future replication.

In the early 1980s, Kolner developed a checklist to improve the MEDLINE search interview process.[3] Most structured database request forms followed a similar format, asking first for identification and payment information, then for a description of the topic accompanied by refinements such as age groups, languages, and years to cover. Additionally, requesters were often asked to sign a waiver indicating their understanding of the costs involved and restrictions on use of the results and releasing the library and/or searcher from liability. These forms were later transformed into electronic versions. They could be completed either by the requester or by the interviewer.

With the rise of the evidence-based medicine movement and its standard of describing clinical questions in PICO format, Booth and colleagues explored ways of revising search forms to include this option.[4] PICO is a mnemonic representing the key components of the question:

P is for patient, population, or problem (i.e., condition of interest).
I stands for intervention (i.e., treatment, diagnostic process, or exposure).
C is for comparison, either its presence or absence to other measures.
O represents desired outcome (e.g., decreased mortality or weight reduction).

Other librarians, for example Snowball[5] and Nguyen,[6] adapted search request forms for residents to include both PICO and narrative. Requiring them to both describe their information need *and* complete a PICO formula compels the learners to think through the research question more thoroughly. After discussing the search together, the librarian and student can decide who will run the search.

Brown has taken the request form a step further.[7] It includes questions to answer not only about the search but also about the types of evidence needed (i.e., types of studies to look for). It also provides tips on how to conduct a research project, reminders of how to perform a good search, and, finally, how to appraise the literature. The form itself (available at www.goo.gl/vbNZbR, accessed on December 8, 2015) contains links to the research guides created by Brown and colleagues at Virginia Commonwealth University to further expand the users' understanding of evidence-based practice. Thus the search request form becomes an educational tool as well as a search tool.

More recently, others have been questioning the "one size fits all" mentality of using PICO for developing every clinically based search.[8, 9] My personal preference is for a narrative from the requester (i.e., a few sentences or a short paragraph describing the information need); then if a PICO is required, we can develop it together. Too often the PICO alone results in a list of possible search terms with little understanding on the part of the requester of how to combine them, or students forcing questions to fit into the mold. The broader description provides greater insight into the requester's thinking about the topic and opens doors for conversation and other paths to follow.

Questions to Ask

Reference interviewers begin with the same questions used by journalists: who, what, when, where, why, and how. Conversations take place around those questions to gather all the information needed, begin strategy development, and educate the end user. The next few paragraphs describe several types of specific questions to ask. As you read through them, think back to our veterinarian. What questions will you want to ask to clarify his request? Ask all of them, a few of them, or different ones depending on what information you need. Each interview and discussion is unique to the requester and the request.

Identification usually comes first. This is the housekeeping part of the negotiation and quickly handled. Who wants the search? Is it the senior researcher or an undergraduate? Someone affiliated with the institution? Contact information is provided. Is she a returning client or someone new to the process? Determining the background of the individual will help gauge the amount and depth of information retrieval needed as well as the amount of education to provide about the process. Additionally, institutions may want to know the departments and categories of staff asking for searches in order to provide targeted marketing or future services.

Is the question or topic stated clearly? Are relationships between concepts identified? Is there a PICO present? Or has the requester provided only a list of words? Having a narrative speeds the process; however, a list can act as a starting point for a useful conversation. Recently, a graduate student came to me and showed me her search strategy, "HIV PrEP Vaccines," and asked why she was retrieving so few articles describing pre-exposure prophylaxis for HIV infections and the use of vaccines to prevent HIV infections. Her short, written strategy provided me with an opportunity to clarify the information she was seeking (by defining "PrEP" and suggesting alternate phrasing and keywords) as well as stating the relationship between the three words she was using ("and" when she meant "or"). I also explained to her how the search system was handling her list and taught her how to construct a search to find the combination she desired. After our initial discussion, we were able to reframe her question into a strategy the PubMed database could use in the way she wanted and examine the search results for keywords. It allowed her to combine her subject expertise with my search expertise for a positive outcome.

Often, asking the client to state an ideal title for the hoped-for results will help clarify his thought process and suggest approaches for you to take. Having the requester define unfamiliar terms or supply synonyms will flesh out the request so that it becomes searchable. This conversation can lead into a discussion about the differences between the use of natural language and controlled vocabulary and how the search results will be impacted depending upon the choice of terms used. Performing a quick Google search at this stage to identify keywords or background information provides an opportunity to educate the user on the difference between database and web searching and what results to expect from each source.

What time period and which languages should be considered? Should the search include patents, abstracts, and reviews or be limited to reports of clinical trials? Are there known articles or authors to look for? What are the requester's expectations for the results? Is she looking for a specific answer (fact or figure) or to compile a lengthy bibliography? Answers to these questions allow you to begin the process of resource selection and develop a tactical plan as well as share with the client possible challenges inherent in the search. In addition, this part of the interview helps determine whether a database search is required or if the information might be found somewhere else. Sometimes just Googling it may be enough. One attribute of expert searchers is that they direct the individual to the most appropriate resource that will satisfy the requester's need, both in terms of information and timeliness.

When are the results needed? This afternoon? Tomorrow? Or is this a long-term project expected to culminate in a systematic review six months to a year out? Because of the immediate gratification provided by web surfing, requesters may need assistance forming realistic expectations around the length of time required for a complete search (as well as the time needed to review and analyze the set of references generated by the search). Once the deadline is negotiated, priorities can be set and the search begun.

Where is the information most likely to be published? Will it appear in the popular or academic literature? Or hidden in statistical reports and dissertations? Are there key journals or authors the search should identify? In what field of study does the topic fall? Is this cutting-edge research or long-standing knowledge? This information is critical in determining which resources to search (i.e., standard bibliographic databases or grey literature resources).

Why is the information needed? Is this to provide background for a grant application? Develop a journal article or a systematic review? Support a clinical or personal healthcare decision? Learning the reasons for the request influences the questions asked, the tactical plan, and the search strategy. Will a "quick and dirty" search with a couple of keywords to uncover a few relevant articles suffice, or is an exhaustive, thorough search required, with multiple strategies and databases to locate as many relevant articles as possible?

How much information is wanted and what degree of relevancy is needed? Is there a maximum number of references the user is willing to review or manage? How will results be delivered? In what format? Are duplicate references acceptable? Can you set up exclusion and inclusion criteria at the time of the search and develop an algorithm for them?

Throughout the interview cycle, you are beginning to develop your tactical plan (i.e., your overall approach to the search) and think about the databases to search and terms to enter. The background information provided is used to consider how a search might be focused or narrowed if the retrieval is too large or expanded if the search results are too few. References that are identified as being exactly what the user wants can be mined to identify other search terms to retrieve more articles like them or find articles that cite the original references. Additional boundaries for the search are chosen during the discussion, such as time period searched, languages, acceptable publication types, age groups, and so on. (The choices will vary depending upon the database selected and the client's needs.) Descriptions of what has already been tried can serve as pointers to new strategies, as background reading for you, or as opportunities to educate a client about the database or search process.

EDUCATION AND SETTING EXPECTATIONS

"Increasingly our role is trying to educate people to the idea that there is no perfect search and you can't fulfill your needs through one search box."[10] This mission is accomplished with explanations of the databases, search strategies, and so on, provided during the pre-search interview and mid-course corrections so that the user becomes aware that there are limitations to the process. An important message to share is that although a search will be as comprehensive as possible (if that is what the client desires), it is impossible to find *all* relevant articles. Articles can, and will be, missed—for example, because they aren't included in the database used, the indexer failed to assign the correct terms, or the searcher overlooked a synonym. The user can, however, help create the balance between precision and recall by being forthright and complete about his information needs as the search unfolds. You can then restructure a search with different terms or try a different database in attempts to increase retrieval. Comparing results from a simple web search to a bibliographic database search or a carefully constructed search strategy against a simple keyword search offers tangible evidence to the requester about the value of multiple approaches and resources.

Building that successful collaboration requires identifying roles for each team member, such as who will perform the search. If a journal article is planned, who will get authorship or acknowledgment? If the librarian is creating the final search strategy, authorship should be requested. The authorship negotiation needs to take place at the beginning of the process to avoid surprises at the end. Realistic expectations around procedures, library policy, and search results are established. By the end of the interview, the requester should have a better understanding of what an expert searcher can do for her.

Coaching Role

As mentioned in the previous chapter, one of those services can be advising on or coaching the requester through the search process. According to the Southern California Online Users Group, the end user needs to acquire "a simple mental model of how the search process works, help in selecting appropriate databases, or an end-run around the selection process, and help in formulating a search query."[11] The conversation during the interview paints the picture of the process for the end user. Discussions of databases and their advantages and disadvantages for the topic or an outright recommendation of the database to use for this search are part of the negotiation. Keywords and strategies may also be shared. How the work is divided (i.e., who does what) should depend on the desires of the user. What will fit her time frame or her learning style?

When the end user comes to you (often referred by an advisor or colleague), first ask specifically how the end user wants to use your expertise. Is it for suggestions of terms or databases to use or instruction in search mechanics and citation management? Then conduct an interview around those responses and identify the extent of the requester's current knowledge. Ask too for the requester's preferred learning style. She may want to be directed to tutorials for self-instruction or prefer to be walked through the process during your consultation or simply handed a search strategy. With that information, you can work together to achieve the desired goal. When the session is complete, send the requester away with resources (e.g., copies of the strategy developed, web sites for additional instruction, or contact information for further questions) to reinforce the lessons learned. Once the end user realizes all that is involved in formulating and running a search, she may contact you to complete the search.

MID-COURSE CORRECTIONS AND POST-SEARCH EVALUATION

If the end user sits with you while the search is run, immediate feedback is provided about the relevancy of the results and the success of the search. Changes can be made on the spot to correct for errors and change directions. More information about this topic will be found in chapter 5, "Search Review and Evaluation."

Both discussions and evaluation forms after the search is completed can provide feedback to you. At the very least, by providing contact information, requesters can return for either revisions, new searches, or additional instruction based on the results and experience.

APPLY THE LEARNING

- Identify the PICO in the following scenario: a resident in rehabilitation medicine is attempting a systematic review of the literature on yoga, more specifically its use in older adults to increase balance and reduce accidental falls.
- Write a list of questions you would routinely ask or create or modify a search request form to meet your needs.
- Think about some recent reference interviews you have participated in. What additional questions could you have asked to build a better picture of your tactical plan? What cautions or information about the process should you have shared with the requester?

NOTES

1. Ross, Catherine Sheldrick, Kirsti Nilsen, and Marie L Radford. *Conducting the Reference Interview: A How-to-Do-It Manual for Librarians.* 2nd ed. New York: Neal-Schuman, 2009.

2. Gawande, Atul. *The Checklist Manifesto: How to Get Things Right.* New York: Picador, 2011.

3. Kolner, Stuart J. "Improving the MEDLARS Search Interview: A Checklist Approach," *Bulletin of the Medical Library Association* 60 (1981): 26–33.

4. Booth, Andrew, Alan J O'Rourke, and Nigel J Ford. "Structuring the Pre-search Reference Interview: A Useful Technique for Handling Clinical Questions," *Bulletin of the Medical Library Association* 88 (2000): 239–246.

5. Snowball, Robin. "Using the Clinical Question to Teach Search Strategy: Fostering Transferable Conceptual Skills in User Education by Active Learning," *Health Libraries Review* 14 (1997): 167–172.

6. Nguyen, Tony. Personal communication. May 2014.

7. Brown, Roy Eugene. "A Checklist on Searching for Evidence and Teaching Evidence-Based Practice," *MLA News* 54 (2014): 10.

8. Bramer, Wichor M. "Patient, Intervention, Control, and Outcome (PICO): An Overrated Tool," *MLA News* 55 (2015): 6.

9. Kloda, Lorie A, and Joan C Bartlett. "Formulating Answerable Questions: Question Negotiation in Evidence-Based Practice," *JCHLA/JABSC* 34 (2013): 55–60.

10. Duke, Lynda M, and Andrew D Dasher, eds. *College Libraries and Student Culture: What We Now Know.* Chicago: ALA Imprints, 2012: 26.

11. Basch, Reva. "Measuring the Quality of the Data: Report on the Fourth Annual SCOUG Retreat," *Database Searcher* 6 (1990): 21.

Chapter Three

Resource Selection and Evaluation

Resource selection is the first step before search terms are chosen and a step-by-step search strategy is developed. Based on their training and knowledge of database content, search engines, interfaces, and semantics, expert searchers analyze the question and select the best tools and resources for the job depending on what is available for the topic of interest and the amount of information desired. For facts and figures, it might be either a web search or databank; for a list of references, a bibliographic database.

As identified in the SLA list of competencies, three skills that characterize information professionals are their in-depth knowledge of many databases and databanks, their ability to quickly review and analyze new or unfamiliar databases for future use, and the use of their judgment to select the best resource for the task. Although this book focuses on bibliographic database searching, many of the suggestions provided in this chapter can be utilized or adapted for use in searching the web or databanks.

WEB VERSUS BIBLIOGRAPHIC DATABASE

Many searches, especially by students, begin with a quick Google (or similar) search. Why? Because it is familiar, easy, quick, free, and, for them, efficient or even second nature. Regardless of the type of material or information sought, a web search is the answer in their minds. And, in reality, it can be a good place to start as well as an excellent means of identifying the amount of information out there. Most search engines examine thousands of resources speedily, filter the results based on search words, and perform some ranking by relevance or other parameters. Inevitably, at least one item in the retrieval will answer the searcher's question, and the individual stops searching once the immediate need is met. He then misses additional relevant, and possibly important, research or information. The sometimes overwhelming amount of retrieval generated by search engines may also cause the end user to settle for the first item that catches his eye regardless of quality, authenticity, or reliability; a phenomenon called satisficing. (Plutchak[1] dubbed these the satisfied and inept users.) One role for the expert searcher is to convince these users to take their request to the next level.

This too easily satisfied group of users continues to concern the expert searcher,[2] as does the novice's overreliance on the web for research. Since the introduction of Google Scholar in 2004, debate has raged in both the library and subject specialty literature about its effective use.[3, 4, 5, 6, 7, 8, 9, 10] The general consensus among these and other articles seems to be that while it is reasonable, and even expected, to use the web as a resource, it should be viewed as an adjunct to database searching. Google can be a good starting point but it should not be the only search. Results should be reviewed and evaluated using the same tools you use with databases.

Thus expert searchers frequently provide information or demonstrations on advanced search techniques to improve results or on the ways in which search engines and databases operate and what they retrieve so that end users become more knowledgeable information consumers. In particular, Haddaway and colleagues constructed a simple chart (figure 3.1) comparing the characteristics of bibliographic databases and search engines,[11] which can be used in teaching students how to determine which resource to use.

Teaching end users how to evaluate retrieval from web resources improves the effectiveness of their web searching. During an interview, the librarian can jump onto the web to discover background information, experts in the field, or search terms, and then show the requester how to leverage those results into a successful bibliographic database search. Often, sitting with the requester and comparing the results pulled from a web search to those from a bibliographic database search will encourage the end user to make better choices. By maintaining a neutral or positive attitude toward web searching as well as offering to assist with the process, expert searchers can turn end users into effective bibliographic database searchers and teach them to use the web to their advantage.

Many researchers and search specialists in the health sciences rely on either PubMed or its subset, MEDLINE, to meet all their search needs for much the same reasons that beginners rely on web searching; these two databases are readily available, easy to use, and familiar, and provide extensive coverage of the biomedical sciences. Searching multiple databases, however, will yield more comprehensive results. Each database contains unique materials that will not be found in the other; as a result, you must search more than one database to attempt a comprehensive search. Additionally, because of the interdisciplinary nature of research, researchers need to select

Feature	Academic Citation Databases	Academic Citation Search Engines
Time coverage	Depends on the database, but time restrictions apply for all (for earliest entry) and may depend on institutional subscription	No time restrictions (full *post hoc* population of records)
Access	Via an online platform for which a subscription is often required (e.g. Proquest)	Service provided purely through a free-to-access online search engine
Inclusion	Typically selectively included according to a predefined list of journals, publishers or subject areas	Anything that matches a set of criteria automatically included. Criteria (for Google Scholar): 1) must have a dedicated page with a title, 2) title must be closely followed by authorship list, 3) manuscript should be PDF, HTML or DOC file, 4) manuscript file should include a 'References' or 'Bibliography' section
Update frequency	Variable–may be as often as weekly, but some databases are monthly or less frequent (e.g. Biological Abstracts, 6 weeks). Updates are based on print versions of journals so will not include 'early view' manuscripts until they appear in print. Updates are based on citations submitted by catalogued journals	Typically 1–2 weeks
Examples	Web of Science, Biological Abstracts	Google Scholar, Microsoft Academic Search
Search facility	Full Boolean strings allowed	Variable–Google Scholar allows limited Boolean operators (no nesting using parentheses permitted) and search string limited to 256 characters
Results displayed	Unlimited results from within the database returned, but numbers estimated for large record sets (> c. 5,000). Results sortable by many different fields	Typically limited–Google Scholar limited to first 1,000 with no explanation of or alteration to sort order

doi:10.1371/journal.pone.0138237.t001

Figure 3.1. Typical Characteristics of Academic Citation Databases and Search Engines. *Source:* Haddaway NR, Collins AM, Coughlin D, Kirk S. *The Role of Google Scholar in Evidence Reviews and Its Applicability to Grey Literature Searching.*

from the larger universe of databases in health, social, and biosciences instead of settling for just one.

In general, bibliographic databases provide the most reliable and effective access to identifying research because of the number of access points provided by the database's structure and interface. The references retrieved can then be used to locate full text, either electronic or print. Relying only on data sets, databanks, or archives of journal articles that do not have added materials such as abstracts, tags, or annotations limits results. Those searches can serve as useful starting points or indicators of the amount of material available, however.

SINGLE SEARCH BOX FALLACY

One of the attractions of using a single search box like Bing's or Google's is the ability to perform federated searching (i.e., the ability to enter a single set of terms and have multiple databases searched simultaneously) on the web. [12] The one-stop-shopping aspect of federated searching saves time and often uncovers material that otherwise would go undiscovered because that particular resource would not have been explored. This capability is especially useful in uncovering the grey literature (i.e., materials that are out of the publishing mainstream).

When licensing or purchasing access to bibliographic databases at an institution, especially for use by end users, librarians often choose to work with a single vendor in order to be able to offer cross-file searching, a form of federated searching. End users enjoy the serendipity factor of stumbling across a reference from an unknown source seemingly at random as well as the freedom from learning multiple interfaces in order to perform comprehensive searches. Vendors and librarians continue to develop discovery tools that work across resources. However, it is incorrect to think that a single search box will yield a completely successful search.

The drawbacks of federated searching, such as the inability to use the unique entry points or search features in different databases as well as the lack of common vocabulary across them, frustrate expert searchers because they are aware of how much may be missed with this approach. For example, in EMBASE, the study type of randomized controlled trial (RCT) is identified with the *subject term* "randomized controlled trial," whereas in MEDLINE the same phrase is classified as a *publication type*. Simply typing in "randomized controlled trial" will only retrieve materials from one database and not the other unless both types of terms are in the default searchable fields for each database. Similarly, features such as automatic mapping of words to indexing terms may be turned off for cross-file searching so that only words in the title or abstract of the article are searched, and not the added keywords, thus losing much of the benefit of searching a structured database instead of the web. Additionally, if the ability to search assigned subject terms is available, different words may be used in different databases for the same concept (e.g., "disabled children" in MEDLINE is "handicapped child" in EMBASE). The problem of multiple word meanings is also an issue in federated searching. What would happen if "adherence" was used as a keyword in BIOSIS (a biological and life sciences database) and PsycINFO (covering psychological literature) at the same time? Very different articles would be retrieved because of the various meanings of adherence (i.e., stickiness vs. staying with a plan).

Because of these factors, most expert searchers prefer to take advantage of the specific access points and search features provided by individual databases in order to produce comprehensive searches. Thus searchers learn to analyze and evaluate databases, looking for the useful features in each one to create the best search for the client. Multiple databases are searched sequentially and other means of eliminating duplicate references are used when compiling the final set of results.

DATABASE SELECTION

During the pre-search interview, database choice is one topic of conversation. Reference librarians as well as expert searchers are expected to be familiar with the details of several databases in order to discuss these options with requesters. How is the choice made as to which database to use, especially if the topic is interdisciplinary in nature? Or for a topic that is unfamiliar to you? Most expert searchers learn the key databases in their subject area and develop a network of colleagues to ask for other topics. A more optimal solution is to use the criteria listed in this chapter to evaluate databases as needed.

The standard go-to suite of databases for biomedical searchers includes MEDLINE or PubMed, EMBASE, CINAHL Plus, Cochrane Library, Web of Knowledge (Web of Science and BIOSIS), and PsycINFO. Often overlooked additional possibilities include CAB Abstracts, National Guideline Clearinghouse, Global Health, ERIC, Scopus, Google Scholar, AMED (an alternative medicine database), and Agricola. When supporting healthcare administration or bioengineering, additional databases such as ABI/Inform, Inspec, or Academic Search Complete should be considered. Patent and legal searching represent another area of expertise and should be left to the experts in those fields. Breaking the habit of relying on one database for all searches is the end goal of learning how to evaluate databases. A quick way to identify possible databases is to visit various library web sites and look at the databases on offer there or at subject research guides provided on the sites.

Grey Literature

Especially for systematic reviews in which the intent is to gather as much information as possible, the grey literature must be considered. "Boiled down to the most basic elements, grey literature is everything but peer-reviewed journals and academically or commercially published books," according to Von Hendy.[13] (This is his interpretation of the standard definition developed at the Fourth International Conference on Grey Literature in Washington, DC, October 1999: "That which is produced on all levels of government, academics, business and industry in print and electronic formats, but which is not controlled by commercial publishers.") Grey literature includes internal reports, dissertations, conference proceedings, world reports, patient education materials, and so on.

As befits its name, grey literature can be difficult to discover. Web or Google searching plays a significant role because of the breadth of web sites examined. Other tools for identifying grey literature include the New York Academy of Medicine's bimonthly publication *The Grey Literature Report in Public Health*, alerting readers to new materials in health services research and public health topics (www.greylit.org/). The Canadian Agency for Drugs and Technologies in Health (CADTH) offers a number of tools for identifying and evaluating grey literature on its web site (www.cadth.ca/resources) as well.

While subject coverage is usually the first consideration in choosing the databases to search, other factors come into play. Knowledge of the available databases at the institution as well as the elements and features of the unit record and interface contributes to the decision. Cost still plays a factor in that budgets may not stretch far enough to license a database. As to how many databases to search, the amount and level of information requested during the pre-search interview determines that.

DATABASE EVALUATION

What are the specifics to look at when evaluating a database? Over the years, various elements have been proposed.[14, 15] A synthesis of these factors, and the ones I find most useful to consider, are listed below. Many of these questions should be asked of web sites and resources as well.

Factor	Description
Credentials	Publisher and contact info
Content	Information provided
Structure	Organization of database
Interface	Tools for using it
Managing Results	Display, save, print
Searcher Support	Help files and services
Quality	Errors, consistency, etc.
Costs and Benefits	Financial and other

Let's look at these factors in more detail. There are no given right or wrong answers for each question. Instead, you need to determine when you might use that database and how you will create your strategy. A thorough understanding of the database informs the interview process by allowing you to set reasonable expectations with the requester, letting her know the strength and limitations of the databases to be used.

Credentials

- Who produces the database or site? Authentication and reputation—what qualifies them to produce this?
- What is the overall aim of the database? Who is its target audience?
- Can you find out more? Is there contact information?

Content

- What information is provided? Is it all from the source material or are there value-added elements such as tags or abstracts? Links to full text? Links to library holdings?
- What sources are covered? Is the item indexed cover to cover or only selected parts?
- What types of publications are included (e.g., books, images, book reviews, proceeding abstracts, journal articles)?
- Is there a list of sources? Does it include periods of coverage?
- What publication years are included? What is the time lag between publication and inclusion in the database? What is the update schedule?
- What countries, languages, and subjects are covered?
- What is its size?
- What is the overlap with other databases?

Structure

- How is the content organized?
- What elements make up individual records? Are they identified and searchable? Are some just for display purposes or internal processing?
- How is the information in the field formatted?
- Are there rules regarding spelling—international or American English?
- Are there rules for authors (e.g., number of authors, identification of first author)?
- Is there a thesaurus or controlled vocabulary? How is it organized? Alphabetically or hierarchically? Are definitions provided?
- What are the default search fields?

Interface

- Is it easy to use and figure out?

- If use is restricted, is there a clear authentication or login process?
- Is it customizable? Are there options for novices and advanced searchers?
- Are there pulldown menus or browsable indexes? Autofill? Mapping?
- Is there a single search box?
- What is available in addition to Boolean logic? Positional operators? Phrase searching?
- Can you truncate? Map to other terms or references?
- Can search terms be limited to specific fields? Multiple fields at once? Pre- or post-qualification?
- What is the processing order for search strategies? Can it be changed, for example, by use of parentheses?
- Are there stop words? Are there ways to work around stop words?
- Are there pre-set filters or limits that can be used? How do you restrict to humans only or specific languages, for example? Or other aspects of interest.

Managing Results

- How are results displayed? Printed? Emailed? Saved?
- Can they be filtered or analyzed? Can duplicates be removed?
- Can they be exported into citation management software? In one step or multiple steps?
- How can search history or strategies be displayed? Saved? Set up for automatically recurring searches?

Searcher Support

- How do you request help?
- What help is available and in what formats? Online tutorials, webinars, telephone, or print?
- Are promotional and marketing materials available? Will representatives come to give presentations?
- Can you get a timely response?

Quality

- Are there errors in the record construction or typographical errors? How are they handled or corrected?
- Is there consistency in indexing (i.e., do similar articles receive like descriptors)? Are thesaurus terms used in the same way by all indexers?
- What is the responsiveness to requests for help or more information?

Costs and Benefits

- What is the cost to license or access the database?
- How does this database compare in coverage to what is already available? Is there enough unique material to justify the purchase or licensure of another database?
- Are there significant value-added features from one vendor that suggest a change in publishers would benefit the workplace?

An additional useful tool for evaluating databases as well as web search engines and other products is the *Charleston Advisor* (www.charlestonco. com; subscription may be required). This publication provides reviews and comparisons of various databases and their interfaces for information professionals in a style similar to that of *Consumer Reports* for household products.

ANATOMY OF A DATABASE

As part of the database selection process, we familiarized ourselves with the database's content and evaluated its structure and contents; that is, we dissected it. In order to create a successful search strategy, you must know exactly what you will get when you type in a word or a phrase. Therefore, you need to identify the default search fields, connections, and processing order for each database (and interface) that you use. Can the defaults be overridden? If so, how? How can the information within specific fields be utilized to best advantage? How can built-in features of the interface work for you? This section looks at the bones (unit record) and skin (interface) of the PubMed database as an example of what to look for during the database dissection. This same careful approach should be taken when examining other databases of interest. Usually, you can find descriptions of this information in the user guide or help section of the database.

Unit Record

The unit record (consisting of bibliographic information, value-added information, and processing notes) forms the basic skeleton of a database. The bibliographic information (i.e., author, title, journal name) is used to display the search results: a list of articles to find and evaluate. Processing notes such as the date the record was last touched are usually for internal use by the publisher rather than searching, although knowing the difference between "in process" and "submitted by publisher" can provide a clue when a search fails. The myriad of access points created by the value-added information from the database producer and/or vendor (e.g., indexing terms) are the building blocks to focus on and manipulate to retrieve the best results. In fact, it is the value-added information that makes computer-based searching so useful. Knowing the elements of the unit record, the format of the searchable fields and data contained within them, along with the rules used in creating the elements making up the unit record allows you to more accurately and efficiently retrieve information as well as to avoid careless mistakes.

For example, students frequently request retrieval of only peer-reviewed articles about their topic. Although "peer reviewed" is a designated journal subset (value-added information) in the CINAHL Plus database, it is not in PubMed. Therefore, a search in PubMed limited to "peer-reviewed" by typing "peer reviewed [sb]" will fail, while it will succeed in CINAHL Plus. (Because the majority of articles in PubMed are from peer-reviewed journals, a workaround can be achieved by constructing a search and removing any publication types, e.g., editorial or letter, that are not be considered to be peer-reviewed items.)

Figure 3.2 lists the fields of the PubMed unit record from the National Library of Medicine. A more complete description with notes about its contents and default search fields indicated may be found on its web site at http://www.ncbi.nlm.nih.gov/books/NBK3827/#pubmedhelp.Search_Field_Descriptions_and. The short table is presented here for easy referral as using these fields in searching is discussed.

Search Field Descriptions and Tags   Go to: ⊙

Affiliation [AD]	Investigator [IR]	Pharmacological Action [PA]
Article Identifier [AID]	ISBN [ISBN]	Place of Publication [PL]
All Fields [ALL]	Issue [IP]	PMID [PMID]
Author [AU]	Journal [TA]	Publisher [PUBN]
Author Identifier [AUID]	Language [LA]	Publication Date [DP]
Book [book]	Last Author [LASTAU]	Publication Type [PT]
Comment Corrections	Location ID [LID]	Secondary Source ID [SI]
Corporate Author [CN]	MeSH Date [MHDA]	Subset [SB]
Create Date [CRDT]	MeSH Major Topic [MAJR]	Supplementary Concept[NM]
Completion Date [DCOM]	MeSH Subheadings [SH]	Text Words [TW]
EC/RN Number [RN]	MeSH Terms [MH]	Title [TI]
Editor [ED]	Modification Date [LR]	Title/Abstract [TIAB]
Entrez Date [EDAT]	NLM Unique ID [JID]	Transliterated Title [TT]
Filter [FILTER]	Other Term [OT]	UID [PMID]
First Author Name [1AU]	Owner	Version
Full Author Name [FAU]	Pagination [PG]	Volume [VI]
Full Investigator Name [FIR]	Personal Name as Subject [PS]	
Grant Number [GR]		

Figure 3.2.   List of PubMed Search Fields and Tags. *Source:* **"Search Field Descriptions and Tags." PubMed Help. Last modified February 14, 2016. http://www.ncbi.nlm.nih.gov/books/NBK3827/#pubmedhelp.Search_Field_Descriptions_and.**

How does familiarity with unit record contents and construction rules affect your searching? Knowing, for example, that up until 2014 author address information in the affiliation field of PubMed was only provided for the first author and that the text was taken as delivered by the publisher, you can explain to an administrative assistant, for example, that it is not possible to run a search that will retrieve *all* articles written by members of the department because of the incompleteness of the information as well as variations in names (e.g., UW, U Wash, Univ Wash, etc.) in the affiliation field. Or when looking for articles written by David Smith with no middle initial (or even with a middle initial), it is necessary to combine an author search with subject and/or address options because full author names were not used in PubMed until 2002. And even then there will be false drops because of the common family name. As ORCID and other means of unique author identification are developed, searching for publications by a specific author may become easier.

Interface

Interface rules determine in which fields words are searched, how submitted search terms are combined, and in what order they are acted upon. Most basic interfaces are built for the infrequent user who enters a phrase, a sentence, or a few words. Systems like Google Scholar and PubMed intentionally construct their interfaces so that you can ask a question in natural language and get useful results. By knowing and using the rules behind the interface, you can improve the search and get better results.

What happens when you enter "measles outbreak" (but use no punctuation) in a search box? It depends. In PubMed, the system assumes that you meant to search the combination of the two words as measles *and* outbreak and not as the specific phrase. Based on the search rules, because no specific fields were designated, the default search fields of title, text word, journal title, and author will be searched *and* all words will be automatically mapped to the equivalent MeSH terms *and* those terms will be exploded for a complete search. In EMBASE or CINAHL Plus, the words are also searched in combination but are not automatically searched as a phrase or mapped to relevant subject headings. These rules then partially account for differences in retrieval when "identical" search strategies are used across multiple databases. (Note: In all three cases, the phrase can be requested by placing quotation marks around it. Additionally, mapping and explosions can be requested in EMBASE and CINAHL Plus by checking a box.)

Search terms can be restricted or qualified to specific fields using a variety of methods. Pre-qualification places designators as the terms are entered (e.g., measles [ti] or measles.ti.) to find the word only in the title of the article. Some interfaces provide checkboxes on the screen, allowing searchers to limit the results to specific fields by clicking on them before the search is run.

Post-qualification (i.e., qualifying search results rather than the initial search terms), can be accomplished in some databases by adding the field identifiers to the search number. Other filters or limits such as language, publication type, or age are often also available to restrict results to specific categories after the fact. Both recall (the number of references) and precision (the relevance of the references) are affected by specifying the fields to be searched rather than relying simply on the default field.

Is there both a basic and an advanced interface available? Most basic interfaces are created for the novice searcher to use and to handle simple searches. With only a few words entered, they are combined in a manner prescribed by the interface rules and results quickly appear. But are the results enough? Or on target? Unless an advanced option, either by use of another screen or the ability to enter qualifiers, is provided, results cannot easily be expanded or narrowed. Another advantage to using an advanced option is that it will often set the stage for easy use of Boolean operators to combine different aspects of a topic. More about this in chapter 4, "Search Strategy Development."

Some database interfaces may offer an autocompletion capability when typing in words or show you a browse or pick list to either expand your selection of search terms or identify correct ones to use. Other databases may alert you to typographical or spelling errors and suggest a corrected search strategy.

Many database interfaces provide links from the search result display to increase retrieval or locate additional materials. For example, authors' names or subject headings may be live links that when clicked retrieve more articles by that author or with that descriptor. Some databases and interfaces provide links for finding "more like this" (look for terms like "find similar articles" or "find related"). The algorithm to retrieve those similar articles varies among databases. In some cases, the relationship is defined by the number of subject headings or keywords that are held in common by both articles. In other databases, the relationship is defined by the references cited by both articles. You need to check the database documentation to view the strategy in use by that database so that you understand and can explain to the requester the results returned when a "related articles" link is followed. Finally, links may also be provided to either the institution's catalog so that location of materials can be determined or to article repositories such as PubMed Central or publishers' web sites so that full text may be retrieved.

Databases and their interfaces are continually revised, so take care to review current rules and documentation before developing a search strategy. Try the exercises below to familiarize yourself with databases. Then consult the next chapter for information on selecting search terms and combining them for retrieval.

APPLY THE LEARNING

- Using the questions from the interviews you considered in chapter 2, identify at least two additional databases other than PubMed or MEDLINE to search.
- Select one of those databases or a database you are less familiar with or are considering licensing and answer the questions listed in this chapter under "Database Evaluation."
- Scan the results when you search "concussion" as an unqualified term, as a MeSH term, or as a word in the title of the article in PubMed (www. pubmed.gov). How are the results affected?

NOTES

1. Plutchak, T Scott. "On the Satisfied and Inept End User," *Medical Reference Services Quarterly* 8 (1989): 45–48.

2. Plutchak, T Scott. "Inept and Satisfied, Redux," *Journal of the Medical Library Association* 93 (2005): 1–3.

3. Kim, Sarang, Helaine Noveck, James Galt, Lauren Hogshire, and Kerry O'Rourke. "Searching for Answers to Clinical Questions Using Google versus Evidence-Based Summary Resources: A Randomized Controlled Crossover Study," *Academic Medicine* 89 (2014): 940–943.

4. Gehanno, Jean-Francois, Laetitia Rollin, and Stefan Darmoni. "Is the Coverage of Google Scholar Enough to Be Used Alone for Systematic Reviews?" *BMC Medical Informatics and Decision Making* 13 (2013): 7. doi: 10.1186/1472-6947-13-7.

5. Chen, Xiaotian, and Kevin O'Kelly. "Cross-Examining Google Scholar," *Reference and User Services Quarterly* 52 (2013): 279–282.

6. Dixon, Lydia, Cheri Duncan, Jody C Fagan, Meris Mandernach, and Stefanie E Warlick. "Finding Articles and Journals via Google Scholar, Journal Portals, and Link Resolvers," *Reference and User Services Quarterly* 50 (2010): 170–181.

7. Bramer, Wichor M, Dean Giustini, Bianca MR Kramer, and PF Anderson. "The Comparative Recall of Google Scholar versus PubMed in Identical Searches for Biomedical Systematic Reviews: A Review of Searches Used in Systematic Reviews," *Systematic Reviews* 2 (2013): 115. doi: 10.1186/2046-4053-2-115.

8. Freeman, Maisha Kelly, Stacy A Lauderdale, Michael G Kendrach, and Thomas W Woolley. "Google Scholar versus PubMed in Locating Primary Literature to Answer Drug-Related Questions," *Annals of Pharmacotherapy* 43 (2009): 478–484.

9. Nourbakhsh, Eva, Rebecca Nugent, Helen Wang, Cihan Cevik, and Kenneth Nugent. "Medical Literature Searches: A Comparison of PubMed and Google Scholar," *Health Information and Libraries Journal* 29 (2012): 214–222.

10. Bramer, Wichor M, Dean Giustini, and Bianca MR Kramer. "Comparing the Coverage, Recall, and Precision of Searches for 120 Systematic Reviews in Embase, MEDLINE, and Google Scholar: A Prospective Study," *Systematic Reviews* 5 (2016): 39. doi: 10.1186/s13643-016-0215-7.

11. Haddaway, Neal Robert, Alexandra Mary Collins, Deborah Coughlin, and Stuart Kirk. "The Role of Google Scholar in Evidence Reviews and Its Applicability to Grey Literature Searching," *PLoS ONE* 10 (2015): e0138237. doi: 10.1371/journal.pone0138237.

12. Baer, William. "Federated Searching: Friend or Foe?" *College and Research Libraries News* 65 (2004): 518–519.

13. Von Hendy, Matthew. "Fifty Shades of Scientific and Technical Grey Literature," *Online Searcher* 38 (2014): 60–65.

14. Bethel, Alison, and Morwenna Rogers. "A Checklist to Assess Database-Hosting Platforms for Designing and Running Searches for Systematic Reviews," *Health Information and Libraries Journal* 31 (2014): 43–53.

15. Allison, DeeAnn, Beth McNeil, and Signe Swanson. "Database Selection: One Size Does Not Fit All," *College and Research Libraries* 61 (2000): 56–63.

Chapter Four

Search Strategy Development

Information gathered during the negotiation cycle is used to develop both the tactical plan and the specific search strategy: one for each database to be searched. The tactical plan is the overall approach to the search—that is, the databases or resources to investigate as well as concepts and broad parameters of the search. It may also include some time to research the topic yourself. The search strategy is the step-by-step plan for retrieving citations.

After the search interview and database selection are complete, you will develop a specific step-by-step strategy that includes deciding on search terms and how to combine them. Although you can just jump in and run a search, aka "just Google it," a more thoughtful, thorough approach to building your strategy will yield the best results. The checklist or search request form used during the interview can serve as the basis of a search strategy worksheet, or you can develop a separate one. If you recall, the form developed by Brown described in chapter 2 specifically asks the requester to suggest possible search terms. Another excellent worksheet is the one developed by Janis Glover at the Cushing/Whitney Medical Library, Yale University (http://doc.med.yale.edu/guides/files/CT_blank_new.docx), for use in system atic reviews. The form shown in figure 4.1 is the one that I use; it has evolved over the years. Although simple, it contains the basics for planning a search. Whichever sheet (or none at all) you use is a personal choice. Bottom line: use the one that best suits your personal preparation style.

In developing the strategy, you move from concept selection to term selection to search term combination. For our veterinarian, what are the concepts of interest? What search terms best express these concepts? This chapter discusses how to find materials on topics by using both natural language and indexing terms. It also provides information about indexing practices and principles, focusing on those used in MEDLINE that make search-

State search topic in the form of a sentence or short paragraph. Indicate key concepts by circling or highlighting words.

Alternatively, state it in PICO format

P (Patient, Problem, Population)

I (Intervention)

C (Compared with)

O (Outcome)

List concepts and limits. Identify synonyms and word variations for each concept (use back of page as needed).

Concept 1

Concept 2

Concept 3

Limits (inclusions and exclusions)

Outline search steps (note databases to use, combinations of terms, possible alternate approaches, etc.).

Figure 4.1.   Search Strategy Worksheet. *Source:* **Created by author.**

ing more successful. I will also review different approaches to building searches.

SEARCH TERM SELECTION

Studies show that students (and novice searchers) only use one or two search terms and expect to get results; in fact, this simplistic approach is marketed by interfaces and search engines using a single search box. Although these end users may be satisfied with their results, with our training, expert searchers know that only the surface has been scratched and more work is needed. Thus it becomes crucial to identify the concepts of interest and the most complete set of search terms expressing those concepts.

Although looking for authors' words (i.e., natural language) is a quick way to retrieve a few relevant articles on a subject, consider, however, how many other articles remain undiscovered because the author used a different word than the one you did. Selecting keywords from a defined list that have been used as assigned subject descriptors will retrieve additional relevant material and improve the search quality, recall, and precision. Combining subject descriptors with natural language will result in an even more comprehensive search.

Natural Language

Sometimes natural language is the *only* way to retrieve very current material when new phrases are coined or new products developed and indexing terms have not yet been added to the thesaurus. Try, for example, "exploding head syndrome" in MEDLINE. That phrase has no equivalent Medical Subject Heading (MeSH) term as of this writing and assigned terms are inconsistent. The unique words used by the author readily identify relevant articles in this type of situation when the only indexing terms available are too general to be of use (in this case, "parasomnia" or "sleep-wake transitions" or "sleep disorders"). Using the most specific or unique words as the first search step may make quick work of a request, especially in clinical situations or when scoping out a topic. The most relevant materials will surface first and further refinement or searching may be minimal.

Another reason to begin with the words suggested by your client is that these terms are the ones that person will look for initially when judging the relevance of the search retrieval. After using the requested keywords, you can follow up and expand the search with synonyms and additional, official indexing terms. This expansion can easily be done by viewing the full record of the citation and making note of both subject headings and authors' words.

What is a word in database searching? In most databases, a word is defined as an alphanumeric character string separated on either end by a space. Hyphenated words can either be compressed (e.g., "self-respect" becomes "selfrespect") or the hyphen replaced with a space (i.e., "self respect"), depending on the rules of that database or database vendor. Similarly, stand-alone numerals may be treated as words, page numbers, or search sets, thus producing unexpected results when used. Sometimes numerals can still be used, if relevant, as a search term by qualifying them with punctuation (e.g., quotation marks) or field abbreviations (e.g., "ti" for "title" as described in chapter 3). Review of the database documentation before creating searches using only natural language will help you avoid these mistakes.

For increased retrieval, consider using truncation to collect word variations such as plurals, adjectives, and alternate spellings. In most systems, wild-card characters such as an asterisk (*) are added at the end of a word fragment (e.g., "adoles*") or inserted in the middle of a word (e.g., "wom#n") to accomplish this task. Be careful when deciding where to place the character. Entering a truncation sign too soon can result in false drops, such as when "labor*" is entered to retrieve "laboratory" or "laboratories," and instead the results also include "laboring," "laborious," and so on. A more effective placement for the wild card in this case would be "laborat*." Or it may be more effective to type in the list of desired words (e.g., "victim" or "victims"), especially if you are just looking for a plural. Some databases will limit the number of variants they will use, so the longer the initial string, the better. Truncating can cause other changes in your search strategy. When truncation is used in PubMed, for example, the automatic exploding of words that are also descriptors and automatic mapping to subject headings are canceled. More information about explosions and mapping is provided later in this chapter when controlled vocabulary is discussed.

Many commonly used single words are designated as stop words and cannot be used for searching. These are frequently occurring words such as "a," "about," "over," and "upon," as well as the names of the Boolean and positional operators used in that interface. Like numbers, sometimes when these are enclosed in quotation marks or entered as a part of phrases they can still be utilized in a search; "exploding head syndrome" is a case in point.

When you choose to use a phrase because it best describes the needed information, think about how to enter it. In most systems, using quotation marks around a string of words will force the system to search it as a phrase. (Note: In most cases, it is actually telling the system to search for this specific string of characters so you usually cannot use truncation wild cards within quotation marks as words are not spelled with them.) However, if PubMed doesn't find a quoted phrase in its phrase index, then the words will be ANDed together and looked for in all the default search fields. The double quotes also turn off automatic mapping and exploding in MEDLINE. The Ovid interface, on the other hand, treats a string of words entered as if they are a phrase and searches in the Ovid default fields for the phrase, so the use of quotation marks is not necessary. Check out the database documentation before proceeding.

Searching by natural language alone will result in moderately successful searches. Because only those words and not general concepts are retrieved, however, it may require several iterations of a search using different words in order to avoid missing relevant materials. Fortunately, most systems, Web of Science being a notable exception, use indexers to review articles and assign keywords from specific lists or thesauri to identify the concepts covered by the article. Some database producers are also experimenting with automated or computer-assigned subject headings for indexing. These search terms or subject descriptors can be used to build more comprehensive searches and improve your search results. You may still need to do iterative searching, but you may not have to do as much of it.

Thesaurus or Controlled Vocabulary

Why should you use a thesaurus? Using natural language alone retrieves only those words, not necessarily the concepts of interest. Utilizing a standardized list of terms that have specific, well-defined meanings to represent a concept lets you retrieve articles on that idea regardless of the differences in vocabulary used by the authors. This list is referred to as a thesaurus or controlled vocabulary and the terms contained within it are called subject headings, descriptors, or subject terms.

Every database usually uses a thesaurus unique to it. Each controlled vocabulary is developed to organize and describe the subject matter of that specific database. As a result, federated searching fails when only descriptors are used for searching; a term that exists in one thesaurus may be different (or nonexistent) in another. Your goal as an expert searcher is to familiarize yourself with the various vocabularies and their meanings.

Thesauri share several common characteristics. Most lists are organized both alphabetically and categorically, often in a hierarchy or outline format that shows relationships between words. The categories indicate connections between the terms; that is, more specific subsets or broader, more general terms. When building the search, you can often specify that all the narrower terms be used in addition to the top umbrella term; this practice is called exploding a search term. Multiple entry terms serve as cross-references and entry points into the thesaurus, leading the searcher to preferred subject headings in the database. Often the interface can map the entry terms to the preferred subject heading so that you need not worry about which descriptor is preferred. Subheadings (i.e., descriptors to further define or group topics) are provided in many databases as well. These subheadings can be linked or attached to indexing terms for searching purposes. The best, and most useful, thesauri provide expanded definitions of descriptors, dates of usage, and allowable subheadings instead of just a long list of words. You can review and utilize this information as you construct search strategies or discuss research questions with your clients.

Well-built interfaces provide a mechanism to search for subject headings that have been designated by the indexer as the main or major focus of the article. Some systems will let you use shortcuts (i.e., abbreviations or codes) or select from a pulldown list to more quickly search as well as avoid keyboarding errors. Database documentation describes the indexing practices for the database as well as how to use controlled vocabularies to best advantage and the specifics of entering them into the interface.

Selecting the descriptors to use in any given search can be done in a variety of ways. Your client may suggest specific subject headings to try. These can be used after checking the thesaurus to determine if they truly will retrieve the concept requested or if there are others that might work better. Another method is to run a quick search using natural language to identify a few relevant articles and examine their assigned descriptors. Recurring terms identified in this way can be used to build another search—again, after looking them up in the thesaurus to understand their meaning and identify additional useful terms. Or, based on the information from the interview, you can prepare a strategy by working with the controlled vocabulary to identify the possible combinations of subject headings and subheadings that will achieve the desired results. Then mine the resulting articles for more terms, either official subject headings or words from the title and abstract, to use in the search strategy.

Medical Subject Headings (MeSH)

MeSH, the controlled vocabulary developed and used by the National Library of Medicine (NLM) to describe the subject content of materials in its databases, is perhaps the most familiar and most heavily used thesaurus in biomedical database searching. Mastering this system will give you transferrable skills for using other vocabularies. Complete information about MeSH can be found on the MeSH web site (www.nlm.nih.gov/mesh). Selected information is provided in this chapter to illustrate thesaurus structure and use by expert searchers. Many other thesauri and databases follow the same practices. The examples provided were accurate as of printing.

Originally developed in the 1960s, MeSH now contains over 27,000 terms and is updated annually to reflect changes in both subject matter and vocabulary. You can look for terms alphabetically or view them in 16 large subject categories (called trees) with more specific terms displayed beneath broader terms. The complete controlled vocabulary can be downloaded from the NLM site but most expert searchers rely on either of the two online versions, the MeSH database (www.ncbi.nlm.nih.gov/mesh) or the MeSH browser (www.nlm.nih.gov/mesh/MBrowser.html). Use the MeSH browser when you want to see complete indexing or application notes and dates and the MeSH database for quick search formulation.

A snapshot of the entry for "text messaging" is shown in figure 4.2. Notice how broader and narrower relationships between terms are graphically depicted through indentations as well as the numbering or classification system for each category. Subject headings may appear in more than one tree as shown by multiple numbers listed with the terms.

MeSH uses subheadings with subject terms to identify the more frequently discussed aspects of a topic, such as therapy of a disease. (Subheadings were originally headers used to subdivide long lists of references on the topic identified by the subject term in the printed *Index Medicus* so that researchers could more quickly focus on citations of interest, since abstracts were not printed in the paper index. Now they serve as a quick way to narrow a search.) Just like MeSH terms, subheadings can also be grouped as families (see below, following figure 4.2).

Text Messaging

Communication between CELL PHONE users via the Short Message Service protocol which allows the interchange of short written messages.
Year introduced: 2012

PubMed search builder options
Subheadings:

- [ ] economics
- [ ] ethics
- [ ] instrumentation
- [ ] legislation and jurisprudence
- [ ] organization and administration
- [ ] standards
- [ ] statistics and numerical data
- [ ] trends
- [ ] utilization

[ ] Restrict to MeSH Major Topic.
[ ] Do not include MeSH terms found below this term in the MeSH hierarchy.

Tree Number(s): L01.143.506.423.906.377.666, L01.178.847.698.300.500
MeSH Unique ID: D060145
Entry Terms:

- Messaging, Text
- Texting
- Textings
- Short Message Service
- Text Messages
- Message, Text
- Messages, Text
- Text Message

All MeSH Categories
   Information Science Category
      Information Science
         Communication
            Language
               Language Arts
                  Writing
                     Correspondence as Topic
                       Text Messaging

All MeSH Categories
   Information Science Category
      Information Science
         Communications Media
            Telecommunications
               Telephone
                  Cell Phones
                     Text Messaging

Figure 4.2.   MeSH "Text Messaging" Record. *Source:* "Text Messaging." MeSH database. Accessed March 17, 2016. http://www.ncbi.nlm.nih.gov/mesh/?term= text+messaging.

Statistics & numerical data[1]

Epidemiology

Ethnology
Mortality

Supply & distribution
Utilization

The name of the family (which is a subheading in its own right) is in bold font with the related terms indented underneath it. In this example for "statistics & numerical data," its related subheadings are "epidemiology," "ethnology," "mortality," "supply & distribution levels," and "utilization." In many cases, if someone is interested in finding statistics on a topic, he will also find numbers in articles about that service's utilization or supply and distribution; thus he would use the entire family of subheadings in his search. Just as headings can be exploded for searching, these subheading families can be exploded to broaden a search. And just like descriptors, subheadings need not be exploded if only the one subheading is of interest.

For most searching, the subheading is directly attached to the descriptor for the best results. For example, the use of antibiotics for animal bites seen in the emergency room would be searched as "bites/drug therapy" AND "antibiotics [pa]." Sometimes, though, to broaden a search you will want to "free float" a subheading, that is, search a subheading as a freestanding term not attached to a descriptor. Searching "chronic disease [mh]" AND "px [sh]" in PubMed, for example, will retrieve articles on the emotional impact of chronic disease on both the family and the patient, whereas "chronic disease/px" will retrieve articles only on the disease's psychological impact on the patient. Free floating a subheading is also one way to locate articles when either an indexer has incorrectly assigned a subheading or a given subheading is not allowed to be used with a descriptor.

Indexing Principles for Articles in MEDLINE

The following indexing principles and rules are true for Medline. Similar practices are in place for other databases and should be reviewed before searching. Subject experts (who receive extensive training) read journal articles and assign the most specific MeSH terms applicable, usually 10 to 12 of them, to a unit record. Using the MeSH vocabulary ensures that articles are uniformly indexed by subject, whatever the author's words. Indexing for each article is based on the entire article rather than just the title and abstract.

Although an average of 10 terms is assigned to each article, there may be as many as 15 or 20 terms or as few as three to five assigned. Articles in the journal subsets of PubMed (e.g., dental journals) or from older years tend to have fewer terms assigned than do more recent ones. Usually, only two or three of these subject headings are chosen and designated as major headings (or the main points) of the article. The rest of the headings are considered to be minor headings and provide more descriptive information about the article. The provision of these additional indexing terms makes online database searching so valuable because there are more opportunities to identify relevant articles. Additionally, you get a richer picture of the article without necessarily reading it.

Articles are indexed to the most specific MeSH term or closest match available. For example, "mouth protectors" rather than the more general term "protective devices" would be used for articles about mouth guards. Articles discussing Pilates, for example, would be assigned "exercise movement techniques" as a heading because it is the nearest match.

Drugs, equipment, and specific tests and products are indexed under their generic names or categories. Trade or brand names may appear in the title, chemical substance, and abstract fields so they still can be used as search terms. Because some citations in PubMed are never indexed, both generic and trade names should be used when searching in order to ensure more comprehensive retrieval. Techniques, methods, and geographical subject headings are usually only available as minor terms or searchable in the title or abstract keywords.

Specialty terms (i.e., words ending in "-ology," "-iatry," "-iatrics") are typically used for articles discussing the discipline or profession rather than subjects managed by the specialty. Exceptions include "physical therapy," "dentistry," and "occupational therapy," which are used for articles about the occupations as well as treatments provided by these professionals.

Additional rules of thumb when either searching or assigning subject headings in MeSH should be applied as follows:

1. Choose a pre-coordinated, single subject heading whenever possible (e.g., "dental care for children" for an article about dental treatment provided to children).
2. Use a heading-with-subheading combination (e.g., "glaucoma/prevention & control" to find articles on some of the preventative measures for glaucoma).
3. Combine two related subject headings (e.g., "tibial fractures" AND "fractures, open" for the topic "open fractures of the tibia").
4. Select two or more unrelated subject headings (e.g., "biopsy" AND "liver" or "liver diseases" for a liver biopsy).

The method of indexing articles, assigning terms, and searching with subject headings described for MEDLINE is similar to that used in other databases. When searching other databases, review their thesauri and indexing rules before beginning.

LIMITATIONS OF THESAURI

Relationships are challenging to express or search for unless a subheading such as "secondary" or a pre-coordinated subject heading such as "prenatal exposure, delayed effects" exists. In these cases, the successive-fraction method of searching may work best, as a large set is accumulated and reviewed for relevance and references are identified by the addition of more terms.

New organisms, conditions, and concepts are discovered and described daily. The controlled vocabulary, which is only revised annually, may not keep pace with the developing language. Using both natural language and controlled vocabulary will enhance your searching.

Indexing consistency has been a concern since databases were developed. Differences in perception and in subject knowledge will provide different approaches to topics and in general; no two indexers or searchers will use identical sets of terms. A principle of indexing may be forgotten or an invalid subheading used. Funk and Reid described the inconsistencies of indexing in 1983.[2] Another study, 20 years later, reported that the consistency rate remained virtually the same.[3] And 10 years after that, another paper indicated indexing inconsistency continues.[4]

Finally, searching with words selected only from the thesaurus limits the search retrieval both to the time period in which the terms are in existence and to articles that already have assigned terms. Unless a narrow search is desired, it is better to search keywords as both descriptors and words in the title or abstract in order to generate greater retrieval and improve recall.

COMBINING NATURAL LANGUAGE AND CONTROLLED VOCABULARY

The two ways of searching complement each other. This approach has been discussed in several articles, including Jenuwine.[5] After deciding on the terms to use, they must be combined in logical ways. This can be accomplished with Boolean logic or positional operators.

You may remember Boolean logic from algebra lessons. These are the combinations that let us combine groups of terms either to merge (OR), intersect (AND), or exclude (NOT or AND NOT) groups (or, in searching, concepts). For example, if I wanted to use several words to describe physical activity I would OR them (e.g., yoga OR sports OR swimming). If I wanted articles that discuss two different concepts, I would AND them (e.g., job satisfaction AND salaries). If I wanted to ignore a segment of the population in my results, I could use "hearing disorders NOT children." Different databases act on Boolean operators in different ways (i.e., processing order). PubMed acts on the Boolean operators from left to right. Other systems use AND first and then OR. Sometimes you can force the desired order by placing groups of terms in parentheses; for example, "wellness AND (yoga OR sports OR swimming)" will get different results than the same words entered without parentheses because the words within parentheses are handled first.

Phrases imply a specific word order. However, sometimes concepts are described in multiple word orders. Positional operators such as NEAR or WITHIN are used to overcome this challenge. This enables retrieval of materials, for example, in which two different phrases to express the same concept, such as "the victims of domestic violence" or "domestic violence victims," are used. A good rule of thumb when using positional operators is to place words within five to 10 words of each other so that they appear in the same sentence because in most systems the proximity operators will not jump over periods. Not all databases offer proximity operators, however, so check before using them. Also see how punctuation and stop words affect the search process in order to avoid surprises in the retrieval. Look too to see if operators can be used when parentheses, truncation, or Boolean operators are in play as well.

Because of the limitations inherent to both natural language and controlled vocabulary searching, comprehensive searches are most successful when these two elements are combined. The PubMed interface is designed so that words entered into a query box are automatically searched as both controlled vocabulary and natural language, which is why I advocate using this interface for MEDLINE searching. (You can still exercise control over the search by using qualifiers if you so choose.) In PubMed, words typed into the search query box are combined (i.e., ANDed together) using automatic term mapping unless you add other Boolean operators or qualifiers. In other words, unqualified terms are first matched, in descending order, to:

- MeSH Translation Table (MeSH terms, entry terms, subheadings, publication types, pharmacologic action terms, UMLS, and substance names)
- Journals Translation Table (full title and abbreviations, ISSN)
- Full Author Translation Table (full author names)
- Author Index

If a match is made, the term is searched in that portion of the unit record and, in the case of full MeSH terms matched, searched both as a MeSH term and as a text word. MeSH terms are automatically exploded. If no matches are found, the phrases are broken apart into individual words and searched in all searchable fields using ANDs to connect them. To see how PubMed translates a request, click on the Details tab after running the search. By qualifying terms (i.e., attaching a field label to the keyword or using the Limit options), terms can be restricted to specific parts of the unit record or limited to key aspects. False drops will still occur because the matching algorithms are not infallible.

The same approach of combining natural language and controlled vocabulary may be used in any database that provides both options. Other interfaces (e.g., EMBASE or CINAHL Plus) offer the option of mapping words or exploring the thesaurus.

SEARCH CONSTRUCTION METHODS

After you've finished framing the question with the requester, gathering all the relevant information, and selecting your search terms, you will need to create the search. With a completed worksheet identifying your concepts, synonyms, limits, and connections in hand, you are ready to run the search. Two common approaches are used in creating a search strategy; both are valid and easy to learn. Some searchers prefer to cast a broad net and whittle away at the results, while others maintain a laser-sharp focus throughout the process. Choosing which one to use is a matter of personal style or preference, and, occasionally, based on the amount of information available or the reason for the search.

Building Blocks

This is the approach used after you've done your homework and found out all you can about the requester's needs. Each concept with its group of relevant terms is considered a building block. Each concept is searched individually and, like a brick in a wall, combined with the others to get results. By keeping each concept separate, various combinations can be tried along the way until just the right results are found. Using the building blocks of exercise, prevention, obesity, and children, you can create a search like the one below (steps 1 through 5).

Step 1   exercise or physical activity or sports

Step 2   prevention or reduce or reduction or impact

Step 3   obesity or fat or obese

Step 4   children or child or teen or teenage or adolescent

Step 5   1 and 2 and 3 and 4

Step 6   nutrition or diet

Step 7   2 and 3 and 4 and 6

Step 8   5 or 7

Step 9   8 and English language

Step 10 9 and review article

Building blocks are most often used by (and recommended for) beginners because they provide an easy means of keeping track of the synonyms as well as not getting lost in the thickets of parentheses. You can see at a glance which terms are being used and combined. This approach is also flexible in that if a new approach occurs to you while searching, you can try it out immediately. For example, when you scan the results from the search above, the researcher has an "aha moment" and asks you to try another approach—the impact of nutrition on obesity. You can then add steps 5 through 8 to achieve a more complete search.

Taking the building blocks, you can remove pieces of them—a process called successive fractions—to get more focused or relevant results or look at just a portion of the citations. Usually, you can still use the Boolean AND rather than the NOT to accomplish this task. In this way, you can improve the specificity of a search. Or limit by publication type, research method, or language. Steps 9 and 10 above illustrate the use of successive fractions.

Another variation identified by Hawkins[6] is called most specific or least faceted method. During the planning process, you identify the concepts that are most likely to yield the most precise results with the fewest steps. You enter these first with the hope that you can finish the search without additional steps (but you are still prepared if you need them).

Pearl Growing

Also known as snowballing, in this method you start with one or two known, relevant references and expand your search based on them, much like an oyster creates a pearl. It's used primarily to increase recall during a search or in the planning stages to determine relevant search terms. It is especially useful when scoping out possible search terms to use.[7]

During the search interview, your client may be able to provide you either with a specific reference or author in the field or an idea of words that would appear in an ideal title. If not, you can run a "quick and dirty" search of your own creation—that is, enter a couple of keywords in the title to find a starting point. Retrieving the records for those references, you can look at the indexing and abstract to find synonyms, descriptors, or other authors to use.

The most widespread application of pearl growing is the use of the "find similar" or "find related" features built into many database interfaces. By clicking on that link, a new search is run based on an algorithm created by the database producer. These results can either be added to the end results or further examined for clues as to how else to search. This is a quick way to increase the number of hits. The help documentation for the database will usually explain the algorithm in depth so that you can modify it for better results if you wish or explain to your client how more references were retrieved.

Cited reference searching, the process of identifying who has cited a reference, is another form of pearl growing. Why do authors cite materials? To give credit to others, to make a comment on an article, to find support for their own ideas. Looking at the language and the indexing of the articles can also give you more hints for ways to search on your topic. It is another easy way to expand your search. Ortuno and colleagues suggest that using the references from the introduction or conclusions will be most fruitful. [8]

The method you start with depends on your own personal comfort and style as well as how much information you've gathered during the interview and initial scoping. Building blocks work best for focusing a search, while pearl growing expands a search. Pearl growing is especially good for new concepts and poorly indexed materials.

APPLY THE LEARNING

- Using the questions generated in the previous chapter, create search strategies for them.
- Find a current journal article of interest to you and select indexing terms for it from a controlled thesaurus. Check your results by finding the article in the database.

NOTES

1. Subheading family adapted from "MeSH Qualifier Hierarchies." *MeSH*. Accessed March 17, 2016. https://www.nlm.nih.gov/mesh/subhierarchy.html.
2. Funk, Mark E, and Carolyn Anne Reid. "Indexing Consistency in MEDLINE," *Bulletin of the Medical Library Association* 72 (1983): 166–183.
3. Marcetich, James, Marina Rappoport, and Sheldon Kotzin. "Indexing Consistency in MEDLINE." Paper presented at the annual meeting of the Medical Library Association, Washington, DC, May 21–26, 2004.
4. Moreno-Fernandez, Luis M, Monica Izquierdo Alonso, Antonio Maurandi Lopez, and Javier Valles Valenzuela. "Consistency between Indexers in the LILAC Database (Latin American and Caribbean Health Science Literature)," *Information Research* 18 (2013), paper 601. Available at http://InformationR.net/ir/18-4/paper601.html.
5. Jenuwine, Elizabeth S, and Judith A Floyd. "Comparison of Medical Subject Headings and Text-Word Searches in MEDLINE to Retrieve Studies on Sleep in Healthy Individuals," *Journal of the Medical Library Association* 92 (2004): 349–353.
6. Hawkins, Donald T, and Robert Wagers. "Online Bibliographic Search Strategy Development," *Online* 6 (1982): 12–19.

7. Sandieson, Robert W, Lori C Kirkpatrick, Rachel M Sandieson, and Walter Zimmerman. "Harnessing the Power of Education Research Databases with the Pearl-Harvesting Methodological Framework for Information Retrieval," *Journal of Special Education* 44 (2010): 161–175.

8. Ortuno, Franciso M, Ignacio Rojas, Miguel A Andrade-Navarro, and Jean-Fred Fontaine. "Using Cited References to Improve the Retrieval of Related Biomedical Documents," *BMC Bioinformatics* 14 (2013): 113. http://www.biomedcentral.com/1371-2105/14/113.

Chapter Five

Search Review and Evaluation

After spending time with the requester to establish goals and expectations for the search as well as making adjustments and changes as the search unfolds, it is always exciting to see the results and judge how closely you met those objectives. What criteria should you use to measure the results? If the search falls short, what can you do to improve it? And finally, when have you done enough?

During the search interview, together you determined the levels of both recall and precision needed for this particular search. Additionally, you may have discussed who would make that judgment call. In answering a clinical question, the focus is usually on getting the most current, most relevant results (i.e., precision). When searching for a researcher, recall (i.e., finding *all* relevant material on the topic), especially in a corporate setting when a new drug is being developed, is key. These researchers are often willing to review (or have you review) peripherally related references to ensure comprehensiveness. Systematic review support is another setting in which recall becomes important.

Precision is the ratio between the number of relevant articles (relevancy defined by the client) and the number of documents retrieved by the search strategy. Recall is the proportion of relevant studies in the database as a whole. In searching, you are always trying to balance precision against recall—that is, the need for specific results against finding everything that might be relevant. Although the requester may want to find everything, you will never be able to find it all. Some reasons include changing vocabulary, coverage of databases, and the amount of time spent on hand-searching. The following sections summarize the possible ways to improve searches that retrieve too few results (improve recall) or find too much that is not relevant (improve precision) as well as how to determine when to stop searching.

SEARCHES WITH TOO FEW OR NO REFERENCES

Check your strategy against the following checklist:

- Misspellings, alternate spellings, and variant endings
- Missing or improperly placed or incorrect qualifiers or parentheses
- Errors in processing order
- Incorrect nesting or missing parentheses or connectors
- Need to develop more synonyms to include by adding in brand names of an instrument or a specific name for the surgical procedure, or using an umbrella or broader term from the thesaurus
- Exploding subject terms (i.e., using additional related terms)
- Dropping the use of proximity operators and using AND instead
- Decreasing the number of concepts searched (i.e., using fewer ANDs or putting greater distance between the words)
- Use of a free-floating subheading
- Use of the related articles link, if available
- Running a cited reference search

Then ask the following questions:

- Was the appropriate database searched? The correct years?
- Did the client expect or hope to find no articles?

Incorrectly keyed or spelled words are common and easily overlooked at the point of entering search terms. A good habit to develop is to review the text before pushing Send or immediately after a search statement results in zero or very low postings. Two other techniques for avoiding this type of error are to create text files, which are carefully edited before saving, of search strategies to copy and paste into a search, or to have someone else with you, watching the screen as the search is entered and letting you know about possible errors.

Alternate spellings for words, such as "centre" for "center," and variable endings (i.e., plurals and other suffixes) should also be considered when low retrieval occurs. Similarly, alternate names can, and as a rule of thumb should, be used for drugs, conditions, and therapies. This is especially important in searching for medications because different databases and countries use different naming conventions. Using the incorrect system in a search will result in zero retrievals unless automatic mapping occurs. Again, reviewing database documentation to determine which word forms or names are used will prevent errors. Using wild-card characters is an efficient way to gather alternate endings or account for different spellings.

When nesting complex combinations of search terms, it is easy to omit or misplace a parenthesis. Fortunately, many database interfaces will alert you to missing punctuation by redisplaying the search request and highlighting missing items or asking "Did you mean . . . ?" One method to avoid this problem is to use the building-block method discussed in the previous chapter, performing the search in individual steps and combining them at the end. This method of combining after the fact makes it easy to make sure ORs and ANDs are in their proper places.

It's easy to enter the incorrect field qualifier (e.g., AD for author address when IN should be used) or omit a qualifier when needed, or to forget which are the default fields, especially when searching multiple databases and using different vendors. Reviewing database documentation and writing out an explicit search strategy will help avoid these problems.

If an article has not yet been indexed or if a subject heading has not been created for a concept, a search that is limited to subject headings alone might miss key articles. Simply ORing in a brand name or title word can often expand the retrieval in these situations. Using a thesaurus term instead of natural language can increase retrieval by searching on the desired concept instead of the specific word. For example, traumatic brain injuries can be called concussions, TBIs, or closed head injuries. Entering the MeSH term "brain injuries" will find all of those articles indexed for that concept, regardless of the term used by the authors.

To increase recall, try either substituting a broader, simpler subject term or exploding a subject term rather than using the most specific one. Especially for older materials, narrower terms may not have been available for the indexer to use, so the only way to retrieve that material is to use the broader concept term. Limiting those results to a specific range of years will eliminate false drops or irrelevant references from the current years when the narrower term came into use and the general term acquired a broader meaning. Indexers may not remember that a more specific term is available and neglect to assign it. Searching by the broader term will retrieve those lost articles.

Searching only on phrases can limit your retrieval. For example, if a search looks for "workplace violence," it will miss articles that use the phrase "violence in the workplace." Substituting ANDs for adjacency or other proximity operators will result in more references (as well as more false drops). If improved recall is the desired result, however, dropping proximity operators will generate more results.

Similarly, reducing the number of concepts or aspects of the condition to be searched (i.e., using fewer ANDs or limits, such as subsets) will increase retrieval. For example, eliminating the age factor in a search (e.g., "treatment of osteoarthritis in adolescents" as opposed to "osteoarthritis treatment") will bring in additional relevant hits because the author may describe the patients as young adults rather than teenagers. Treatments for adults may very well be applicable to adolescent patients.

Subheadings attached to concepts focus a search. When using therapeutic subheadings, for example, attaching a subheading to a specific condition ensures that the article is about the therapy of that disease and not of another coexisting condition. Just as with assigning subject headings, indexers can either omit subheadings or assign subheadings incorrectly, or it may be unclear which subheading should be attached to which term. In these situations, using free-floating subheadings (i.e., ANDing in subheadings instead of attaching them) can increase retrieval. This technique would work well, for example, when searching for the psychological impact of ALS on the family. If you searched as "ALS AND px AND family" instead of "ALS/px AND family" you would increase the number of relevant hits. In this way, materials will be retrieved regardless of whether the subheading for psychological aspects is attached to the disease or to the family member.

As described in the previous chapter, using the pearl-growing method of searching by following related article links or looking for articles that cite an article that was retrieved will usually expand the retrieval. The full indexing for relevant articles can be displayed and additional subject terms chosen for searching. Some systems will offer clickable links in the display so that you can immediately try out a new term. Or other interfaces will let you start adding to the current strategy.

Did you search both the right database and the appropriate years? If you are looking for abstracts of papers presented at a conference, PubMed will fail because meeting proceedings are not included. You should try a database such as BIOSIS Previews or EMBASE instead. To provide comprehensive coverage, often several databases will need to be used, especially in fields where multiple types of care providers are involved. For example, the rehabilitation of veterans with prosthetic limbs most likely would require searching in CINAHL Plus, PsycINFO, and PubMed at the very least. Additionally, some topics are researched heavily for a while, then set aside as interests or priorities change. If a researcher fails to dive into the older literature, she may not pursue the best future avenues.

Finally, check with the requester to determine if the number of results is what she expected. Researchers may be requesting a scoping search to identify how much has been published and on what aspects of the topic. Or they may be wanting to begin a new line of investigation or submit a patent or funding application and be satisfied with a low retrieval. Often they will not share this with you during the interview because they want to minimize bias and construct a thorough, wide-ranging search.

SEARCHES WITH TOO MANY REFERENCES

Unless they have asked for a systematic review in which as many relevant references as possible are required, most requesters are overwhelmed if they have a large retrieval—that is, over 100 or so references. If you want to narrow the results, try the following:

- Decrease the number of synonyms by using a more specific word, such as the brand name of a medication instead of the generic one.
- Look for words in key fields such as title by attaching a qualifier.
- Use a term from the database's thesaurus or controlled vocabulary, especially if a word could have multiple meanings.
- Attach a subheading to a subject heading to focus the search.
- Tag one or two subject headings as major concepts (i.e., the main point of the article).
- Use a phrase or proximity operators instead of ANDing keywords together.
- Increase the number of search concepts such as age groups or languages or different aspects of the topic and ANDing them together.
- Exclude or limit to specific publication types, journals, or journal collections.

Simply eliminating some of the synonyms will decrease retrieval when keywords are used rather than subject headings. This technique is particularly useful when looking for a particular test, medication, procedure, or piece of equipment. By entering the name of the product (e.g., "C-leg" instead of the more general "artificial leg" or "lower limb prosthesis"), the search results are limited to the named product.

Because successful comprehensive searches take advantage of all the access points of a unit record, often articles that are of less interest or apparently irrelevant will be retrieved unless limits are specified. A quick way of narrowing the search is to specify that certain words appear in the title of the article. (In some systems, you can also turn on a highlighting feature so that when you review the search results, you can see at a glance what terms brought in the record. This can help you decide which fields or terms to eliminate later.)

Using a term from the database's thesaurus can reduce retrieval, especially in situations where a word may have multiple meanings. For example, entering the word "veteran" in ERIC without qualifiers will retrieve articles on military veterans as well as individuals who are longtime employees (e.g., veteran teachers). Searching with the specific ERIC term "veterans" will eliminate the false drops. Similarly, adding a subheading to an indexing term (e.g., "breast neoplasms/diagnosis AND self-examination" instead of "breast neoplasms AND self-examination") will improve precision by ensuring that the articles are retrieved on topic, in this case about performing self-exams to spot possible breast cancer. Identifying "breast neoplasms/diagnosis" as the major concept of the article will further reduce the number of results retrieved and make the search more precise because only those articles dealing with the diagnosis of breast cancer are retrieved.

Using proximity operators such as ADJ (adjacency) or NEAR instead of ANDs to connect words can make a search much more precise. Searching "school ADJ uniform," for example, instead of "school AND uniform" can restrict the results to articles about the benefits of requiring students to wear uniforms instead of the application of uniform guidelines for grading in school.

By using the building-block method of searching step by step and combining in new parameters (or building blocks) such as publication types, languages or years, or subjects, a search can be narrowed. These publication types, years and languages, and so on can either be added to the search to restrict the results or NOTed out to eliminate specific publication types.

FILTERS AND LIMITS

Useful tools to either focus or expand searches are filters or limits [1] (longtime searchers may call them hedges, a term they used to differentiate a collection of terms on a subject from the MeSH trees). The Health Information Research Unit at McMaster University, Canada, in particular has led the way in developing filters for identifying evidence-based research. In addition to developing a collection of terms, the department has conducted tests to test the validity and usefulness of these groupings and has published its findings. Other groups such as CADTH, Cochrane Collaboration, ECRI, and the Inter-TASC Information Specialists' Sub-Group develop filters as well; more information about their resources may be found in chapter 8.

PubMed's Clinical Queries feature and topical subsets are also examples of filters that have been developed and validated over time. Within PubMed Help, links are provided so that you can review these terms. Most of these hedges and filters consist of combinations of natural language and thesaurus terms. By using a predetermined set of terms for part of the search, the searcher can spend more time on the other aspects of the search. I also find the thoroughness of these filters inspires me to be more comprehensive in my own selection of terms.

WHEN CAN YOU STOP?

Searchers always struggle with this decision. Aspects to consider include the following:[2]

- Is the search intended to quickly answer a clinical question? Get an overview of the field? Create a systematic review?
- Are you seeing the same references despite changing your strategy or database?
- Is each new search returning fewer references?

During the interview, these questions will have been discussed and both of you will have determined an acceptable ending point.

After evaluating the search results and trying the different options described earlier in the chapter to adjust them, if you are both satisfied that no additional references are turning up, then you can stop. One way of recognizing an ending point is when the same references are appearing in each of the databases searched or with each different strategy used. A good rule of thumb is to search at least two different databases for relevant material. As discussed in chapter 3, "Resource Selection and Evaluation," each database contains unique material. Thus a search of only one database will fail to come close to retrieving all the information on a topic.

Another factor in completing the search is the amount of effort or energy either party is willing to put into the quest to find information. Often, end users will be "satisficers" and settle for good enough instead of perfect. As an expert searcher, you may want to continue on. You need to weigh the needs of your requester against your time.

EVALUATING SEARCHES

Reviewing search results for precision and recall is only part of the evaluation process, however. Other aspects of the search process need to be examined as well. Evaluation becomes an iterative process throughout the search and is not conducted as an afterthought.

The first evaluation occurs as the initial references are retrieved. By displaying titles and abstracts and reviewing them immediately, you check for keywords previously identified or matches against known relevant articles to verify the precision and relevance of the search. Discussing search results and strategies with the client during the search gives you additional feedback about the quality of the search and increases your knowledge of the topic, which might be utilized either in a future search or in another iteration of the current search. With each new search or revision created, run, and reviewed, you develop a better understanding and appreciation of the various database contents, structure, and interfaces.

Peer review of searches is another possibility.[3] McGowan and colleagues undertook a study to review and update previously published guidelines for peer review.[4] Their work evaluated the suggested elements and recommended retaining the following six items to consider: 1) translation of the research question, 2) Boolean and proximity operators, 3) subject headings, 4) text word searching, 5) spelling, syntax, and line numbers, and 6) limits and filters. Some guidelines or protocols such as those for the European Network for Health Technology Assessment[5] for systematic reviews include a requirement for this type of review. Other searchers choose this mechanism to facilitate their lifelong learning. Everyone approaches topics from different levels of experience and knowledge. An outsider looking at the search request and strategy from a perspective different from yours might suggest a new, and more fruitful, approach to the request, another way of accomplishing the same or similar task in the future. (Remember, however, that you may need to maintain confidentiality of a request; it is a good idea to ask your client's permission to consult with other searchers if needed.)

Evaluation may be informal and accomplished during a conversation without a checklist or form. You can also give requesters an evaluation form or ask them to take a survey after the search is complete and they have had time to use the results. In general, I have found that if a search isn't meeting their needs, the person will speak up at the time, and a follow-up isn't necessary unless your institution requires it for performance reviews or statistical purposes.

NOTES

1. Wilczynski, Nancy I, Ann McKibbon, and R Brian Haynes. "Search Filter Precision Can Be Improved by NOTing Out Irrelevant Content," *AMIA Annual Symposium Proceedings* (2011): 1506–1513.

2. Booth, Andrew. "How Much Searching Is Enough? Comprehensive versus Optimal Retrieval for Technology Assessments," *International Journal of Technology Assessment in Health Care* 26 (2010): 431–436.

3. Sampson, Margaret, Jessie McGowan, Elise Cogo, Jeremy Grimshaw, David Moher, and Carol Lefebvre. "An Evidence-Based Practice Guideline for the Peer Review of Electronic Search Strategies," *Journal of Clinical Epidemiology* 62 (2009): 944–952.

4. McGowan, Jessie, Margaret Sampson, Douglas M Salzwedel, Elise Cogo, Vicki Foerster, and Carol Lefebvre. "PRESS Peer Review of Electronic Search Strategies: 2015 Guideline Statement," *Journal of Clinical Epidemiology* (2016). pii: S0895-4356(16)00058-5. doi: 10.1016/j.jclinepi.2016.01.02.

5. EUnetHTA. *Guideline: Process of Information Retrieval for Systematic Reviews and Health Technology Assessments on Clinical Effectiveness.* 2015. http://www.eunethta.eu/sites/5026.fedimbo.belgium.be/files/2015-07-13_Guideline_Information_Retrieval_final.pdf.

Chapter Six

Search Documentation and Management of Search Results

What is the searcher's role in managing the results? This can range from strictly hands-off to education to hands-on. This chapter discusses options for documenting the search, updating references, and tracking the references.

DOCUMENTING SEARCH RESULTS

One of the key roles for librarians (i.e., searchers) identified in the Institute of Medicine (IOM) standards was documentation of the search strategy, especially when the client will be submitting this to a journal. Search strategies are to searchers what methods are to scientists. Providing the steps used to get to the references lets others replicate the process and verify the findings against their own search (or experiment, to continue the analogy).

Librarians and researchers alike struggle with reporting and documenting searches. A working group of information specialists discussed current practice and conducted a survey to gain insight on this issue.[1] The overwhelming challenge has been the lack of guidance provided by journals. Most librarians and many of the key organizations developing systematic reviews rely on the PRISMA guidelines[2] as the standard for documentation and reporting of searches. You will also find many discussions in the literature of various professions explaining how to track and document searches. During the interview, it is helpful to ask what standard the client is using or if she will be submitting the results to a specific journal so that you can plan ahead for the documentation.

There are presently two main schools of thought in documenting the search strategy. Some prefer to have the entire strategy written out in one long string (sentence) that someone could enter into a database to re-create the search. The challenge with this method is that it is sometimes difficult to follow the parentheses and see that all aspects were covered. Others will share the entire strategy, step by step; although it is long, it makes it easy to see how the search was put together. It also has the advantage that if terminology changes, it is easy to substitute new words or make changes into it. Others will compromise and have relatively long search statements for each concept and show how they are combined. See below for representations of these styles for the question of drug-resistant tuberculosis in homeless or transient populations.

One-Step Strategy Documentation

((mycobacterium tuberculosis [mesh] OR "mycobacterium tuberculosis" OR tuberculosis [mesh] OR tuberculosis OR tb) AND (tuberculosis, multidrug-resistant [mesh] OR drug resistance, microbial [mesh] OR "drug resistant" OR "drug resistance") AND (homeless persons [mesh] OR homeless* OR transients and migrants [mesh] OR transient OR transients OR "street people")) AND eng [la]

Step-by-Step Strategy Documentation

SS 1	mycobacterium tuberculosis [mesh]
SS 2	"mycobacterium tuberculosis"
SS 3	tuberculosis [mesh]
SS 4	tuberculosis
SS 5	tb
SS 6	#1 OR #2 OR #3 OR #4 OR #5
SS 7	tuberculosis, multidrug-resistant [mesh]
SS 8	drug resistance, microbial [mesh]
SS 9	"drug resistant"
SS 10	"drug resistance"
SS 11	#7 OR #8 OR #9 OR #10
SS 12	homeless persons [mesh]
SS 13	homeless*
SS 14	transients and migrants [mesh]
SS 15	transient
SS 16	transients
SS 17	"street people"

SS 18   #12 OR #13 OR #14 OR #15 OR #16 OR #17

SS 19   #6 AND #11 AND #18

SS 20   #19 AND eng [la]

Mixed-Strategy Documentation

SS 1   mycobacterium tuberculosis [mesh] OR "mycobacterium tuberculosis" OR tuberculosis [mesh] OR tuberculosis OR tb

SS 2   tuberculosis, multidrug-resistant [mesh] OR drug resistance, microbial [mesh] OR "drug resistant" OR "drug resistance"

SS 3   homeless persons [mesh] OR homeless* OR transients and migrants [mesh] OR transient OR transients OR "street people"

SS 4   #1 AND #2 AND #3

SS 5   #4 AND eng [la]

Although in theory you should be able to easily replicate the search if you are provided with the strategy, this is not always the case. If you use a different vendor than the original search (or even a different database), you will need to make adjustments in qualifiers and connectors. If much time has passed since the original search was performed, vocabulary may have changed and new terms will have to be added. Therefore, documented search strategies need to be taken with a grain of salt and treated as a starting point. All databases have a mechanism for you to view the steps you took to get the results you send to your client. These can easily be captured with screenshots or in many cases downloaded and saved to either a text or an Excel file. These text files can be revised to present the results in the desired format. In some databases, you can create an account on the system and save the strategy in an electronic format to that account, which can then be used for future searching. These are all easy ways to document the search. These steps can be referred to when writing up the article that uses the results.

AUTHORSHIP

Journals often require authors to provide the search documentation as part of the methods for the article. Here too there is no standardization. You will read articles that simply state a PubMed search was run on the topic. Other articles will include, often as an appendix, the full-blown strategy. Credit (i.e., authorship) for the strategy is often an issue. Too many times the scientist or clinician provides the strategy without acknowledgment of the librarian. This too is a topic that should be negotiated up front during the reference interview. If the strategy is built primarily by the librarian, authorship credit should be acknowledged. Not all librarians publish in other ways, so this work product becomes a means of recognizing a librarian's intellectual contributions to research.

UPDATING SEARCHES

As part of the interview, you will also have discussed whether this is a one-shot search or if the individual is interested in receiving regular updates on the topic. If the latter, again, most systems allow you to set up an account to save the strategy and have it set up for repeat searching on a designated schedule. Instead of using your own account for this, you should assist requesters in setting up their account so that the search can move with them and they can make changes as needed. And they will need to make changes. Remember, vocabularies are usually updated annually. If terms are changed, then the search strategy needs to be changed as well. The client may also move to another institution. If the search is on PubMed, that will not be a problem as that database is available to all. The client's new institution may not have access to other databases, and you should advise her to save a print copy of the strategy before leaving so that she can re-create it on another system. It too will be subject to the problems of changing vocabulary and different interfaces.

MANAGING REFERENCES

If there are only a few references, the client usually takes them and does what he will with them. However, if the retrieval is large and the client is preparing a journal article, meta-analysis, or systematic review of the literature, she will want to keep track of them in a more formal way. In addition to saving the bibliographic information about the article, she will want to note its keywords and where and how to get the full text, and make annotations around inclusion and exclusion criteria for the article as well as its applicability to the article. Usually the client will also want to remove duplicate references, preferably at the time of search but it may need to take place after the fact.

The options for managing references can be overwhelming. Some individuals decide on Excel,[3] which lets you set up tables of references and create separate fields for the bibliographic information and the indexing tags as well as notes about the contents, URLs for the references, and so on. Different worksheets can be created for those articles that are included or excluded and can contain the search strategy. Excel has the advantage in that it is a program readily available and most can use it at this level without additional training. It does have the drawback, however, that when you want to use the reference, you will have to cut and paste it into the manuscript. For this reason, many turn to programs called citation or reference managers.

Using reference managers is most efficient because they provide easy ways of removing duplicate citations as well as inserting references (in the desired format) into documents you may be creating to discuss the references. Some programs will allow you to search databases directly as well as search PDFs you may have acquired during your searching. Using reference manager software to search databases is somewhat controversial. In effect, you are layering one interface over another, and unless the search is quite simple, errors easily occur. For accurate searching, using the database's interface is still the most reliable method. [4]

Deciding on the reference manager to use is definitely a moving target. *Nature*[5] published a recent article describing options, and many libraries (as well as the ubiquitous *Wikipedia*) provide information on selecting the reference manager that is right for you. Proprietary systems for a fee are available (e.g., EndNote or RefWorks[6]) as well as open source programs such as ReadCube or Zotero. Because all accomplish many of the same tasks, you should pick one, familiarize yourself with it, and use it. Other factors in the decision might depend on which one your colleagues use or which one your institution either provides or supports. These programs should be evaluated much the same way a database is evaluated. Here are features you should review to make a choice:

- Cost
- Open source or proprietary?
- Web based?
- Is there an app?
- Ability to insert formatted citations into a document
- Availability of citation styles
- Ability to access and edit offline
- Ability to insert, search, and annotate PDFs

The expert searcher's role in reference managers is usually to assist users in selecting the one that best fits their needs. This means keeping an eye on the literature and trends in systems as well as providing support in the form of workshops, consultations, and handouts on the use of these programs. On the other hand, in corporations there is often the expectation that the librarians will take the lead in managing references even to the extent of reviewing and annotating the literature. This is a proactive value-added role that information professionals can take on to demonstrate their worth to employers.

DEDUPLICATION OF RECORDS

Deduplicating collections of references is another arena where the librarian can provide value-added services to the search process.[7] Prior to beginning a search, you will want to discuss with the client the overlap in database coverage that makes duplicate citations inevitable. Often, the client will want to remove these references before adding them to your collection. Unless the searches are run against databases from the same vendor, this may not be possible. Instead, you will have to rely on some of the reference managers described above.

APPLY THE LEARNING

- Write out the search strategy for one of your searches in the style that you prefer.
- Choose a reference manager, using the questions from before. Try creating a short document with it.

NOTES

1. Rader, Tamara, Mala Mann, Claire Stansfield, Chris Cooper, and Margaret Sampson. "Methods for Documenting Systematic Review Searches: A Discussion of Common Issues," *Research Synthesis Methods* 5 (2014): 98–115.

2. Moher, David, Alessandro Liberati, Jennifer Tetzlaff, and Douglas G Altman. "Preferred Reporting Items for Systematic Reviews and Meta-Analyses: The PRISMA Statement," *PLoS Medicine* 6 (2009): e1000097. doi: 10.1371/journal.pmed.1000097.

3. Brennan, David. "Simple Export of Journal Citation Data to Excel Using Any Reference Manager," *Journal of the Medical Library Association* 104 (2016): 72–75.

4. Fitzgibbons, Megan, and Deborah Meert. "Are Bibliographic Management Software Search Interfaces Reliable? A Comparison between Search Results Obtained Using Database Interfaces and the EndNote Online Search Function," *Journal of Academic Librarianship* 36 (2010): 144–150.

5. Perkel, Jeffrey M. "Eight Ways to Clean a Digital Library," *Nature* 527 (2015): 123–124.

6. Havill, Nancy L, Jennifer Leeman, Julia Shaw-Kokot, Kathleen Knafl, Jamie Crandell, and Margarete Sandelowski. "Managing Large-Volume Literature Searches in Research Synthesis Studies," *Nursing Outlook* 62 (2014): 112–118.

7. Kwon, Yoojin, Michelle Lemieux, Jill McTavish, and Nadine Wathen. "Identifying and Removing Duplicate Records from Systematic Review Searches," *Journal of the Medical Library Association* 103 (2015): 184–188.

Chapter Seven

Current Picture and Future Directions

The landscape for expert searchers is constantly changing. In the early years of database searching, only trained librarians performed searches. As databases opened up to the end user, expert searchers also became coaches, mentors, and educators. With today's reliance on finding the evidence, healthcare practitioners have once again turned to the expert searcher for assistance. As this book goes to press, expert searchers can take on any number of roles. [1, 2, 3] This chapter discusses some possible roles and services librarians can and do offer, future directions for expert searching, and maintenance and improvement of search skills.

SEARCH SERVICES AND EDUCATION

Many libraries offer search services for their patrons. These can be stand-alone enterprises or incorporated as part of the research and consultation (i.e., reference or liaison) services offered by many libraries. Education around database searching may take the form of formal classes, informal coaching, handouts, or tutorials.

Search Services

When offering search services, two of the first decisions to make are:

1. Whether to incorporate the service into standard reference, clinical, or consultation services or to set up a separate operation
2. Whether or not to charge for the service

In both cases, another consideration is the institutional culture. Questions to ask yourself include the following: What are the expectations and needs of my library clients? Are fee-based or recharge services the norm in your institution? Can your budget absorb the costs (publicity, database licenses, staff training, and staff time) of database searching? Do you have staff that are trained to provide quality searching? Is there enough demand for mediated searches that it can be a stand-alone operation? Some libraries compromise and offer coaching and simple searching at no charge and charge for the more comprehensive searching needed for systematic reviews or major research projects.

Systematic Review Search Services

Much of the impetus behind the rise of the expert searcher in recent years has been the emphasis on conducting and sharing systematic reviews. Librarians have become involved in supporting these reviews by writing search strategies and helping manage references. What is a systematic review? It is a review of the evidence, not just the literature on a topic.[4] "Information retrieval for systematic reviews needs to be performed in a systematic, transparent and reproducible manner."[5] To my mind, a hallmark of an expert searcher is that she extends the same energy and care into any searching that she might for a systematic review.

Multiple studies have shown the benefit of involving librarians in the creation and implementation of systematic reviews.[6, 7] Jewell and Gibson succinctly described nine steps they used to build a systematic review service:[8]

1. Develop forms and instructions for the process and complete them together.
2. Use existing standards and guidelines such as PRISMA (www.prisma-statement.org).
3. Register your protocol.
4. Ask for librarian authorship.
5. Create a peer group of librarians to consult and review search strategies.
6. Encourage the inclusion of grey literature in the search.
7. Use reference management software to track the references.
8. Provide training to researchers on critical analysis of articles.
9. Create an updating mechanism for the search.

Note that their steps identify multiple, substantial roles for librarians—database searching, writing, data management, and teaching—as well as provide for collaboration and partnership with clients.

Education

Spending time during the search process to educate the client about database contents and database searching helps set realistic expectations on the part of the client. This education occurs at multiple stages of the search process—during the marketing and publicity of search services, during the search negotiation process, and during the review and evaluation of results.

Education can be as simple as informing the client about the resources to use, the coverage of the database, and how the search engine works. By providing the client with sufficient background information about the search process (i.e., the steps and costs involved and the expected results), searchers can avoid potential misunderstandings.

Formal teaching is offered in many libraries as in-class lectures, classes for credit, or separate workshops on how to use databases. It may also include the development and publication of tutorials, guides, or fact sheets made available 24/7 on institutional web sites. These instructional tools can be supplemented by materials from the vendors. Librarians are often able to take those materials and put them into context for practices at their institution. Adult learning is more successful when the materials can be applied and the students can see the immediate application of the tools.

Coaching someone through a search by advising on strategy formation or term selection is another type of education. The session usually reinforces the complexity of searching and showcases the librarian's knowledge and skill in performing searches. With that realization, clients can become more successful in their own searches by taking advantage of the tips provided. Often, as a result of a coaching session, they will turn to librarians earlier in the process in the future or even ask that the librarian take over the search. These "just in time" sessions may be more successful than the overview lecture at the beginning of the quarter.

MARKETING OUR SKILLS AND SERVICES

Apart from mastering the skills and knowledge needed to become expert searchers, librarians face another challenge when providing quality search services to requesters. Often we are struggling against the mind-set of "I can do it myself" or "Everything I need is on the web—for free." What can we do as librarians to overcome these attitudes?

Much of it comes down to careful marketing of our skills and services as well as proving our worth. Two major library associations, the American Library Association and the Medical Library Association, have conducted studies and collected resources for librarians to provide this evidence. Their web sites (www.ala.org and www.mlanet.org) contain a wealth of material to assist librarians in making their cases. Both organizations and other groups provide classes, discussions, and other opportunities for librarians to develop skills in statistics and publicity as well as learn effective marketing techniques such as creating an elevator speech.

Marketing, either formal or informal, truly is the key to success for search services. In this day of information overload, fliers and emails often go overlooked. I've found word of mouth from satisfied customers (as well as guidelines requiring consultation with a librarian such as the IOM report) to provide the most benefit.

FUTURE DIRECTIONS FOR SEARCHING

Further Expansion of Systematic Review Services

As the demand for systematic review searching continues to climb, librarians are looking for more efficient ways to help produce these specialized searches. This includes refining documentation and reporting guidelines, and creating mechanisms for peer review and sharing of information. Currently, systematic reviews are selected to be updated and new searches run at that time. Researchers are looking at developing living systematic reviews[9] whereby new evidence and research are evaluated as they appear. More exploration of text mining as a means of identifying both keywords and controlled vocabulary to build searches[10] is in our future as well.

Automatic Indexing

Exploration into options for automatic indexing and automatic search building continues, along with ongoing development in database search interfaces. (See "Search Tools" in the next chapter for some examples.) These tools are applications of the snowballing or pearl-growing methods of searching. Additionally, searchers create and share new filters and hedges.

Author Identification

Research into identifying authors by providing them with a unique identifier to better connect authors with their work is ongoing. One promising system, ORCID (Open Researcher and Contributor Identifier), is gaining traction. Some publishers and funding agencies are now requiring authors to obtain these identifiers and provide them with their submissions. If searchers are able to use them when looking for work by specific authors, then the problem of false drops because of duplicate names will be solved.

Increased Searching of Grey Literature

Librarians are learning to utilize nontraditional bibliographic databases to go the extra mile of finding evidence—in particular, searching clinical trials databases to locate data for research trials and searching web sites of organizations and companies to identify published and unpublished reports, as well as listings of abstracts and posters from conferences and meetings. Going first to the web for this type of information is a valid tool for finding information. Librarians play a role here by teaching the individuals to evaluate the information they find on the web, helping them identify criteria to measure the accuracy and validity of the information uncovered.

New Publication Types

Scoping reviews as a form of knowledge synthesis are becoming increasingly popular.[11] This type of review, which provides a broad overview of a topic, is one answer to the steady deluge of evidence. Scoping reviews serve to provide an overview of the topic and direct one to further analysis. Similarly, other groups are looking at creating rapid evidence reviews.[12] Just like the early days of systematic reviews, however, definitions, methods, and reporting mechanisms are fuzzy and in a state of flux. It will be interesting to see how these play out.

EVALUATING AND MAINTAINING SEARCH SKILLS

In order to take advantage of these new directions as well as keep your skills current, you should create a plan for yourself. A first step might be to spend some time on self-reflection. Where do you think you shine and where do you struggle? Maybe you have search mechanics down but need ideas for selecting subject headings. The results from this self-evaluation can suggest areas on which to spend time. The evaluation can also be used as a basis for discussion during annual performance conversations or when creating a professional development plan with a mentor.

A variety of options are available to maintain or develop search skills. This section describes options in general terms. Key specific resources are described in chapter 8, "Search Tools and Learning Resources."

Using search skills constantly by performing searches on a regular basis is the single best way to maintain skills. Ready reference searching—that is, quickly dipping into a database to verify a citation or locate a piece of information requested as part of a reference question—provides another opportunity for practice. This type of searching offers the expert searcher a chance to use old, familiar databases as well as spend time exploring an infrequently used database to identify when and how it might be used for more comprehensive searches in the future. You might volunteer to serve as the document delivery or interlibrary loan department's citation verification person, following up on any complicated citations that are presenting a challenge to the staff. Participating in a campus-wide or multi-institution chat reference service provides another opportunity to explore unfamiliar subjects and databases.

Conducting demonstrations, teaching workshops on databases and search techniques, either to potential clients or colleagues, or coaching new searchers reinforces and improves your own search skills. In the process of preparing for the session, knowledge of database structure, contents, vocabulary, and interface is refreshed. Additionally, questions asked during the session may prompt you to look at the database in another way or follow up on an unfamiliar topic.

Attending in-service trainings, workshops, or classes rather than teaching a session also provides opportunity for learning and skill practice. Additional search training can build new skills or add to existing ones. Opportunities exist in several formats and venues: through vendors, professional associations, and library and information schools as well as in-house training by colleagues or vendors. Increasingly, database providers and organizations are offering web- or video-based training so that instruction may take place when and where needed without incurring travel costs. These may be archived and available for future viewing. Information gained through these opportunities can be used to hone your own skills as well as adapted to educational sessions you provide for your clients.

Attendance at conferences and meetings during which database searching is discussed or demonstrated provides new ideas and information. These sessions may be in the form of formal workshops, presented papers, informal round tables, or vendor demonstrations. The hands-on trainings or demonstrations provided by vendors or at professional meetings are usually of more value to experienced searchers than courses taught at information schools because the academic courses, by nature, are usually more theoretical. Networking with fellow attendees enlarges your learning circle. You could even create a journal club or online discussion group to follow up on topics of interest. Networking online through the use of blogs and discussion groups is another mechanism for tracking changes in database searching or finding help with searches.

Peer review of searches, usually within an organization, offers another approach for exchanging database searching information. The librarians of the Evidence-based Practice Centers have published specific guidelines for peer review of search strategies.[13] Developing a support group of colleagues and seeking out an experienced searcher as a mentor are other means of obtaining feedback about search skills. Working with other experienced searchers provides a source of knowledge and expertise from which to learn.

Reading is also a means of extending one's knowledge base and skills and will supplement practice, meetings, and classes. The database documentation or user manuals, either online or printed, contain a wealth of information and search tips for study and application. Context-sensitive online help is especially useful so that the issue or problem can be seen as it occurs in real life. Newsletters from database publishers and vendors alert searchers to changes in software and databases that affect searching on their products. Making a practice of periodically looking for updated materials is a good habit to form. Some libraries assign the responsibility for following trends in databases and sharing that information with colleagues to one of their staff members. Consider creating a profile or email alert to run automatically against some databases (e.g., PubMed, Web of Science, Inspec, or Library and Information Science Abstracts) that provide coverage of database searching to discover new articles about expert searching.

And don't forget to keep your subject knowledge up to date. Attending lectures, grand rounds, and classes as well as reading in subject areas increases background knowledge that can be used to discuss topics more intelligently with clients and build comprehensive searches. Watch for interesting health topics in newspapers or other media. Reading the articles themselves provides background information that can be used in constructing searches or answering reference questions. Creating and running searches on questions raised from these sources offers more opportunities to practice search skills and identify additional readings. These topics also provide material to create practice exercises for students; adult learners especially respond well to real-life scenarios and will more readily grasp the value of searching when these are presented during demonstrations or classes.

NOTES

1. Tan, Maria C, and Lauren A Maggio. "Expert Searcher, Teacher, Content Manger, and Patient Advocate: An Exploratory Study of Clinical Librarian Roles," *Journal of the Medical Library Association* 101 (2013): 53–72.

2. Rethlefson, Melissa I, M Hassan Murad, and Edward H Livingston. "Engaging Medical Librarians to Improve the Quality of Review Articles," *JAMA* 312 (2014): 999–1000.

3. Perrier, Laure, Ann Farrell, A Patricia Ayala, David Lightfoot, Tim Kenny, Ellen Aaronson, Nancy Allee, Tara Brigham, Elizabeth Connor, Teodora Constantinesu, Joanne Muellenbach, Helen-Ann Brown Epstein, and Ardis Weiss. "Effects of Librarian-Provided Services in Healthcare Settings: A Systematic Review," *Journal of the American Medical Informatics Association* (2014). doi: 10.1136a,oakm;-2014-002825.

4. "Keeping Up with . . . Systematic Literature Reviews." American Library Association, January 25, 2015. http://www.ala.org/acrl/publications/keeping_up_with/slr (accessed January 27, 2016). Document ID: e7e83547-4ca7-1724-e543-30021693ec65.

5. EUnetHTA. *Guideline: Process of Information Retrieval for Systematic Reviews and Health Technology Assessments on Clinical Effectiveness.* 2015: 8. http://www.eunethta.eu/sites/5026.fedimbo.belgium.be/files/2015-07-13_Guideline_Information_Retrieval_final.pdf.

6. Koffel, Jonathan B. "Use of Recommended Search Strategies in Systematic Reviews and the Impact of Librarian Involvement: A Cross-Sectional Survey of Recent Authors," *PLoS One* 10 (2015): e0125931. doi: 10.1371/journal.pone.0125931. eCollection 2015.

7. Rethlefsen, Melissa I, Ann M Farrell, Leah C Osterhaus Trzasko, and Tara J Brigham. "Librarian Co-authors Correlated with Higher Quality Reported Search Strategies in General Internal Medicine Systematic Reviews," *Journal of Clinical Epidemiology* 68 (2015): 617–626.

8. Jewell, Sarah, and Donna S Gibson. "Nine Steps to a Systematic Review Service," *MLA News* 54 (2014): 11.

9. Elliott, Julian H, Tari Turner, Ornella Clavisi, James Thomas, Julian PT Higgins, Chris Mavergames, and Russell L Gruen. "Living Systematic Reviews: An Emerging Opportunity to Narrow the Evidence-Practice Gap," *PLoS Medicine* 11 (2014): e1001603. doi: 10.1371/journal.pmed.1001603. eCollection 2014.

10. AHRQ White Paper. *EPC Methods: An Exploration of the Use of Text-Mining Software in Systematic Reviews*. In press August 26, 2016. Available at http://www.effectivehealthcare.ahrq.gov/search-for-guides-reviews-and-reports/?pageaction=displayProduct&productID=2115.

11. Colquhoun, Heather L, Danielle Lefac, Kelly K O'Brien, Sharon Straus, Andrea C Tricco, Laurie Perrier, Monika Kastner, and David Moher. "Scoping Reviews: Time for Clarity in Definition, Methods, and Reporting," *Journal of Clinical Epidemiology* 67 (2014): 1291–1294.

12. AcademyHealth. *Rapid Evidence Reviews for Health Policy and Practice: A Brief of the Rapid Evidence Review Project*. https://www.academyhealth.org/files/publications/AH_Rapid%20Evidence%20Reviews%20Brief.pdf (accessed February 3, 2016).

13. Relevo, Rose, and Robin Paynter. *Peer Review of Search Strategies*. Methods Research Report. Prepared by the Oregon Evidence-based Practice Center under Contract No. 290-2007-100572. AHTRQ Publication No. 12-EHC068-EF. Rockville, MD: Agency for Healthcare Research and Quality, June 2012. http://www.effectivehealthcare.ahrq.gov/reports/final.cfm.

Chapter Eight

Search Tools and Learning Resources

SEARCH TOOLS

Several groups and organizations have created handbooks, guidelines, or collections of filters as well as other tools you can use to improve your searching. Many university libraries have created guides to producing systematic reviews, among them McGill, Dartmouth, and Yale.

The Cochrane Handbook is used by authors of Cochrane systematic reviews. (Higgins, JPT, and S Green [eds]. *Cochrane Handbook for Systematic Reviews of Interventions*. Version 5.1.0 [updated March 2011]. The Cochrane Collaboration, 2011. Available at www.cochrane-handbook.org.) See especially part 2, chapter 6, which provides instructions on planning and documenting searches.

Finding the Evidence: Literature Searching Tools in Support of Systematic Reviews (https://www.cadth.ca/resources/finding-evidence) is a collection of tools from the Canadian Agency for Drugs and Technologies in Health (CADTH). *Grey Matters* is a checklist of sources and tips to use them for finding grey literature. CADTH's *Peer Review Checklist* for search strategies is a framework for reviewing search strategies. *Strings Attached* is CADTH's collection of filters used in creating its systematic reviews and may be useful for other searching.

Health Knowledge Refinery, McMaster University, Canada (http://hiru. mcmaster.ca/hiru/HIRU_McMaster_HKR.aspx), is a collection of information about projects from the Health Information Research Unit of McMaster concerning retrieval and evaluation of evidence. Of particular interest are the hedges that can be used to focus results on evidence-based materials. This work has been adapted by PubMed to create its Clinical Queries and Special Queries features. Using these strategies as the basis to develop one's own search plan will help ensure comprehensive retrieval. In addition, these guidelines and strategies offer a gold standard that searchers can aspire to and use for self-instruction.

The ISSG Search Filters Resource (https://sites.google.com/a/york.ac.uk/issg-search-filters-resource/home) not only is a collection of search filters but also provides information about appraising and using search filters. ISSG is the InterTASC Information Specialists' Sub-Group, a group of information professionals supporting the research groups who provide technology assessments to the National Institute for Health and Care Excellence.

The MedTerm Search Assist database (www.hsls.pitt.edu/terms/) was developed by the librarians at the University of Pittsburgh to provide a space for librarians to share keywords and search strategies.

Search Builder 1.0 is a Microsoft Excel–based tool to generate, archive, and share search strings for PubMed and EMBASE searches. For more information and a link to download, see Kamdar, Biren B, and Pooja A Sha. "A Novel Search Builder to Expedite Search Strategies for Systematic Reviews," *International Journal of Technology Assessment in Health Care* 31 (2015): 1–3.

The Systematic Review Assistant–Deduplication Module (SRA-DM) is open source software developed at the Bond University Centre for Research in Evidence-Based Practice. For more information on, access to it and its capabilities, see Rathbone, John, Matt Carter, Tammy Hoffmann, and Paul Glasziou. "Better Duplicate Detection for Systematic Reviewers: Evaluation of Systematic Review Assistant–Deduplication Module," *Systematic Reviews* 4:6 (2015). doi:10.1186/2046-4053-4-6.

The Yale Mesh Analyzer (http://mesh.med.yale.edu) is a simple yet effective tool to review and harvest MeSH terms to create a search. You simply enter up to 20 PMIDs in the search box and it produces an Excel chart of the terms so that you can see at a glance the common and unique terms. You can then consider using them in your search.

LEARNING TOOLS

Professional Development section of MLANet (www.mlanet.org): Lists a variety of educational opportunities either offered or approved by the Medical Library Association as well as links to other continuing education (CE) opportunities. Includes a searchable database of courses approved for MLA CE credit hours, which can be used toward membership in MLA's Academy of Health Information Professionals.

"Expert Searchers" column in MLA's newsletter: Appears on a quarterly basis. The column features tips and tricks from expert searchers.

Expert Searching Email Discussion list (http://pss.mlanet.org/mailman/listinfo/expertsearching_pss.mlanet.org): Managed by the Public Services Section of MLA, this moderated list provides a forum to discuss the role of health sciences librarians in expert searching and to share tips and tricks, as well as to ask questions about database searching and explore the role of librarians in training future health sciences librarians and end users in searching best practices.

HLWIKI International (http://hlwiki.slais.ubc.ca/index.php/HLWIKI_International): An open global encyclopedia with portals on health librarianship (including one on expert searching), social media, and information technology topics. Curated by a group of international health librarians.

MEDLIB-L (under the Communication section of MLANet): An unmoderated list providing a forum for MLA members and other health sciences information professionals to discuss issues about health sciences libraries and librarianship. Often includes discussions on expert searching. Little duplication with the Expert Searching Email Discussion list.

NN/LM Training Office (NTC) (http://nnlm.gov/ntc): National Network of Libraries of Medicine (NN/LM) web site describing the training efforts by NN/LM. Includes a calendar as well as links to training materials. Once you have taken the PubMed for Trainers course, you can join the monthly online meetings to share and discuss challenging searches and changes in the databases.

NLM-Announces (https://www.nlm.nih.gov/listserv/emaillists.html/): Provides notification of new and updated files on the NLM web site containing information that impacts searching.

NLM Technical Bulletin (www.nlm.nih.gov/pubs/techbull/tb.html): Offers the most comprehensive coverage of MEDLINE searching. This newsletter includes search hints, reviews system features, and covers data and indexing issues for NLM databases.

BIBLIOGRAPHY

Throughout the book, I have cited references to support some of my recommendations and suggestions. There are a few items that are worth calling out separately here, which you may want to consider reading in their entirety.

Badke, William. "Mythbusting: Seven Google Myths That Complicate Our Lives," *Online Searcher* 38 (2014): 22–26. Well-reasoned opinion piece on why expert searching is challenging in the Google age.

Bell, Suzanne S. *Librarian's Guide to Online Searching*. 3rd ed. Santa Barbara, CA: Libraries Unlimited, 2012. Good basic, general guide on searching.

Booth, Andrew. "Unpacking Your Literature Search Toolbox: On Search Styles and Tactics," *Health Information and Libraries Journal* 25 (2008): 313–317. Helps you examine and develop your own search style.

Harmeyer, Dave. *The Reference Interview Today: Negotiating and Answering Questions Face to Face, on the Phone, and Virtually*. Lanham, MD: Rowman & Littlefield, 2014. Collection of scenarios to help develop good search interviews.

Jankowski, Terry Ann. *The Medical Library Association Essential Guide to Becoming an Expert Searcher: Proven Techniques, Strategies, and Tips for Finding Health Information*. Medical Library Association Guides. New York: Neal-Schuman Publishers, 2008. Emphasis on health-related searching.

Keisure, Barbie E. "Business Databases," *Online Searcher* 38 (2014): 15–20. How to evaluate business databases.

Laserre, Kay. "Expert Searching in Health Librarianship: A Literature Review to Identify International Issues and Australian Concerns," *Health Information and Libraries Journal* 29 (2012): 3–15. International perspective on expert searching.

Liberati, Alessandro, Douglas G Altman, Jennifer Tetzlaff, Cynthia Mulrow, Peter C Getszche, John PA Ioannidis, Mike Clarke, PJ Devereaux, Jos Kieljnen, and David Moher. "The PRISMA Statement for Reporting Systematic Reviews and Meta-Analyses of Studies That Evaluate Health Care Interventions: Explanation and Elaboration," *PLoS Medicine* 6 (2009): e1000100. doi: 10.1371/journal.pmed.1000100. Description of the PRISMA guidelines.

McGrath, Jacqueline M, Roy E Brown, and Haifa A Samra. "Before You Search the Literature: How to Prepare and Get the Most Out of Citation Databases," *Newborn and Infant Nursing Reviews* 12 (2012). doi: org/10.1053/j.nainr.2012.06.003. Background of search request form in chapter 2 as well as additional information to help the end user search.

Sampson, Margaret, Jessie McGowan, Carol Lefebvre, David Moher, and Jeremy Grimshaw. *PRESS: Peer Review of Electronic Search Strategies*. Ottawa: Canadian Agency for Drugs and Technologies in Health, 2008. How to utilize peer review in evaluation of search strategies. Describes the first work on how to utilize peer review in evaluation of search strategies. More updated information is available in chapter 5.

Appendix A

 **MEDICAL LIBRARY
ASSOCIATION**

65 East Wacker Place • Suite 1900
Chicago, Illinois 60601-7298
PHONE 312.419.9094
FAX   312.419.8950
EMAIL info@mlahq.org
WEBSITE www.mlanet.org

Medical Library Association Policy Statement

Role of Expert Searching in Health Sciences Libraries

Introduction

The nation's health sciences librarians must continue to play a significant role in the expert retrieval and evaluation of information in support of knowledge- and evidence-based clinical, scientific, and administrative decision making at all health institutions. The nation's health sciences librarians also have a responsibility to train future health sciences practitioners and other end users in the best retrieval methods for knowledge-based practice, research, and lifelong learning and to help them identify which information needs should be addressed by expert searchers.

This policy statement:
- defines expert searching and provides the background on the issue;
- articulates the role of health sciences librarians in the provision of expert searching; and
- identifies a number of high-impact areas in which consultation and expert searching are critical to the success of the institution.

Definition of Expert Searching

Expert searching in the context of this policy document is a mediated process in which a user with an information need seeks consultation and assistance from a recognized expert. The recognized expert performs a search that is the combined and synergistic application of the following key skills and knowledge:
- ability to accurately identify an information need through effective personal interaction and to clarify and refine the need and retrieval requirements;
- subject domain knowledge and sensitivity to the professional information within the domain to place an information need in the context of a discipline or practice;
- ability to perceive the implications of the information need through relevant institutional knowledge and placement of a request in the context and mission of the institution;
- ability to identify and search resources beyond the electronically available published literature, including the older published literature, gray literature, unpublished information, and Web documents;
- ability to recognize personal searcher limitations related to subject domain or resource specificity as well as the limitations of available institutional resources;
- knowledge of database subject content, indexing or metadata conventions, and online record format to determine relevance to the information need and the method of retrieval access;

- expert knowledge of retrieval system interfaces to determine appropriateness of one interface over another;
- expert application of retrieval system logical, positional, and weighting capabilities;
- ability to be mindful and reflective; to think about and observe what is being retrieved through the use of an iterative and heuristic search process for discovery of relevant evidence;
- ability to use both deductive and inductive reasoning combined with subject domain knowledge to respond to a desired outcome, not necessarily to a literal request;
- ability to efficiently and effectively evaluate retrieved evidence to determine closeness of fit to requestor's recall and precision requirements, expectations, or subject domain familiarity;
- ability to expertly process retrieval for results presentation through removal of irrelevant material from search results, application of data mining techniques to identify themes and gaps in retrieved information, and performance of other editing procedures aimed at optimizing and economizing the subsequent work by the end user; and
- ability to effectively document the search process for end user information or retention for legal purposes.

Health care professionals and biomedical research personnel generally do not have this combined set of skills and knowledge. It remains the province of highly trained and experienced librarians, and is applicable to other important areas requiring expert consultation and training such as:
1. provision of expert consultation to end-user searchers;
2. design of online searching education programs;
3. provision of expert consultation for a health care informatics application;
4. provision of the highly specialized services such as clinical medical librarian programs or clinical or research information specialist in context programs;
5. design of gold-standard searches and expert "hedges" for use by colleagues and end users; and
6. design of expert searching continuing education courses or other peer-to-peer education opportunities.

Background
From its beginnings in the late 1960s through the middle of the 1980s computer-based searching was nearly the exclusive province of medical librarians specially trained in this skill. Training included not only instruction in the somewhat arcane syntax of the command-based language, but more importantly, a thorough grounding in the knowledge of the specialized subject headings used in the databases themselves and the policies that governed the application, manipulation, and coordination of the individual data fields. Although the National Library of Medicine's MEDLINE database was often the first database with which medical librarians became familiar, they were able to transfer their searching skills and analytic expertise to other databases that soon became available via commercial vendors or via internal computer systems. The formal online training programs sponsored by NLM also served as a form of credentialing system for medical librarians responsible for providing mediated subject searches at their respective institutions. During this early period, physicians, researchers, and students who wished to take advantage of the power and

convenience of computer searching were in most cases required to consult a trained librarian. The librarian's responsibility was to refine and clarify an initial research or clinical issue so that it could be effectively translated into the language and logic of a retrieval system. The process of refinement and clarification was repeated as often as necessary to achieve useful search results and could involve the active participation of the researcher or clinician during the search planning and online interaction phase.

Searching performed by trained librarians at academic institutions, including the nation's academic health center (AHC) libraries, was supplanted quickly in the late 1980s by end-user searching as database vendors developed user-friendly search interfaces. The number of online searches increased tremendously, first, as a result of this welcoming user-friendly environment and, second, as the databases themselves became readily available over the Internet. In this new environment, the role of the academic medical librarian in the online retrieval process was transformed from that of trained mediated searcher to online instructor and consultant. Many of the nation's hospital libraries have continued to offer expert literature search services as well as clinical medical librarian services requiring expert literature searches, and have become online instructors and literature consultants to assist end-user searching demands.

Librarian's Role Transformed

The transformation from expert searcher to consultant and online instructor has had both positive and negative aspects. On the positive side, the ubiquity of databases on the Internet and the ease of searching make online searching convenient and efficient for many end users. Highly trained librarians are no longer required as intermediaries for straightforward searches that can be done effectively by end-user searchers; on the other hand, the results obtained by untrained or unsophisticated end-user searchers in the present environment are often of questionable quality at best and dangerous at worst. End-user searchers unfamiliar with a subject domain will not be able to determine what relevant references have been missed or whether they have retrieved the most relevant and accurate information to answer their information need. In some cases, less than expert searching is quite acceptable to end users who only want a few recent references or who are looking for a key citation. On the negative side, librarians who are not required to perform expert searches or expert consultation soon lose the knowledgebase and skill sets required if these skills are not exercised in other ways, such as support of in-depth reference questions requiring literature research, database collection development, and curriculum support. The end-user driven Web and Internet provide end-user searchers with the illusion that they can find anything, even in the gated and highly structured resources so familiar to librarians.

Recently, the increased emphasis on evidence-based practice by the Institute of Medicine has created a renewed interest in the knowledgebase and skill set required for expert literature searching and expert consultation. Librarians are being recruited to join clinical and research teams as clinical medical librarians and information specialists in context and to provide expert consultation on issues ranging from informatics literacy to evidence-based medicine classes. All require the same knowledgebase and skill set identified for expert literature searchers. The emphasis on evidence-based practice, along with publicity about the need for more vigilance about the quality of literature searching following the unfortunate death of a healthy research volunteer at Johns Hopkins, have underscored the need for this policy document.

Where Knowledge Matters Most in Decision Making

It is well known in research that the results of a well-planned, expert literature search often creates the rationale for conducting a new research study (Has it ever been done before? Is it fundable?) and uncovers extant published knowledge related to the new study's proposed methodology. What has become clearer with the emphasis on evidence-based practice is that published evidence is also a critical success factor in the clinical, administrative, and information technology settings of hospitals and academic health centers.

A number of high-impact areas continue to benefit from rigorous examination of the published evidence prior to decision making. The use of evidence- or knowledge-based information retrieved through the expert searching process can help ensure the clinical, administrative, educational, and research success and positive performance of the individual health care provider as well as the hospital or academic health center.

High-impact areas include:

- Complex or unusual clinical cases: Effective management of complex cases almost invariably involves a review and ongoing evaluation of the published evidence.
- Research design support: Assistance with discovering relevant prior work related to a proposed research study or clinical trial will help refine the research problem, identify methodological techniques, uncover contradictory findings, discover alternative animal models, and avoid duplication of effort through effective use of existing knowledge.
- Support of basic science research: Expert identification and application of databases and other tools in the areas of molecular biology and genetics is used to support researchers in the basic sciences.
- Institutional support of patient safety: Support of the institution's efforts at ensuring patient safety including institutional review board (IRB) activities will be assisted by expert literature consultation. IRB staff and committee members may need assistance or training in evaluating the adequacy of the literature search portion of proposed research studies to ensure patient safety. Hospital patient safety committees may need expert search consultation to support the monitoring and resolution of operational issues related to patient safety.
- Institutional support of litigation: Legal actions related to health care institutions including depositions by health care professionals may involve discovery of relevant biomedical evidence through the expert literature search process.
- Key business and academic decisions: An expert search of the published and unpublished evidence may uncover knowledge that will have as great an impact on positive outcomes as a hired consultant. Support of new product line development, recruitment and retention of staff, and other business areas will benefit from the knowledge discovery process. Academic decisions related to promotion and tenure and research productivity will be better informed through the expert search process, in particular through the use of citation searching and journal impact factors.
- Support of scholarship and grant applications: Sophisticated literature research to discover published precedents and prior art is key to success in this area.

- Best practice identification and development: Expert consultation on search methodology and ongoing current literature alerting is used for continuous improvement projects and for constructing best practice guidelines.
- Evidence-based interfaces to the electronic medical record (EMR): Expert consultation is used on search methodology and literature evaluation.
- Patient education support and information therapy: Identification of high quality, authoritative lay health materials in support of patient education is used.

FINAL DRAFT
(4/20/03; revised 6/24/03; revised 8/15/03; revised 8/29/03; revised 9/3/03)

Appendix B

STANDARDS — MARCH 2011

INSTITUTE OF MEDICINE
OF THE NATIONAL ACADEMIES

Advising the nation • Improving health

For more information visit www.iom.edu/srstandards

Finding What Works in Health Care
Standards for Systematic Reviews

These standards are for systematic reviews of comparative effectiveness research of therapeutic medical or surgical interventions

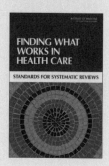

FINDING WHAT WORKS IN HEALTH CARE

STANDARDS FOR SYSTEMATIC REVIEWS

Standards for Initiating a Systematic Review

STANDARD 2.1
Establish a team with appropriate expertise and experience to conduct the systematic review

2.1.1 Include expertise in the pertinent clinical content areas

2.1.2 Include expertise in systematic review methods

2.1.3 Include expertise in searching for relevant evidence

2.1.4 Include expertise in quantitative methods

2.1.5 Include other expertise as appropriate

STANDARD 2.2
Manage bias and conflict of interest (COI) of the team conducting the systematic review

2.2.1 Require each team member to disclose potential COI and professional or intellectual bias

2.2.2 Exclude individuals with a clear financial conflict

2.2.3 Exclude individuals whose professional or intellectual bias would diminish the credibility of the review in the eyes of the intended users

STANDARD 2.3
Ensure user and stakeholder input as the review is designed and conducted

2.3.1 Protect the independence of the review team to make the final decisions about the design, analysis, and reporting of the review

STANDARD 2.4
Manage bias and COI for individuals providing input into the systematic review

2.4.1 Require individuals to disclose potential COI and professional or intellectual bias

2.4.2 Exclude input from individuals whose COI or bias would diminish the credibility of the review in the eyes of the intended users

STANDARD 2.5
Formulate the topic for the systematic review

2.5.1 Confirm the need for a new review

2.5.2 Develop an analytic framework that clearly lays out the chain of logic that links the health intervention to the outcomes of interest and defines the key clinical questions to be addressed by the systematic review

2.5.3 Use a standard format to articulate each clinical question of interest

2.5.4 State the rationale for each clinical question

2.5.5 Refine each question based on user and stakeholder input

STANDARD 2.6
Develop a systematic review protocol

2.6.1 Describe the context and rationale for the review from both a decision-making and research perspective

2.6.2 Describe the study screening and selection criteria (inclusion/exclusion criteria)

2.6.3 Describe precisely which outcome measures, time points, interventions, and comparison groups will be addressed

2.6.4 Describe the search strategy for identifying relevant evidence

2.6.5 Describe the procedures for study selection

2.6.6 Describe the data extraction strategy

2.6.7 Describe the process for identifying and resolving disagreement between researchers in study selection and data extraction decisions

2.6.8 Describe the approach to critically appraising individual studies

2.6.9 Describe the method for evaluating the body of evidence, including the quantitative and qualitative synthesis strategies

2.6.10 Describe and justify any planned analyses of differential treatment effects according to patient subgroups, how an intervention is delivered, or how an outcome is measured

2.6.11 Describe the proposed timetable for conducting the review

STANDARD 2.7
Submit the protocol for peer review

2.7.1 Provide a public comment period for the protocol and publicly report on disposition of comments

STANDARD 2.8
Make the final protocol publicly available, and add any amendments to the protocol in a timely fashion

Standards for Finding and Assessing Individual Studies

STANDARD 3.1
Conduct a comprehensive systematic search for evidence

3.1.1 Work with a librarian or other information specialist trained in performing systematic reviews to plan the search strategy

3.1.2 Design the search strategy to address each key research question

3.1.3 Use an independent librarian or other information specialist to peer review the search strategy

3.1.4 Search bibliographic databases

3.1.5 Search citation indexes

3.1.6 Search literature cited by eligible studies

3.1.7 Update the search at intervals appropriate to the pace of generation of new information for the research question being addressed

3.1.8 Search subject-specific databases if other databases are unlikely to provide all relevant evidence

3.1.9 Search regional bibliographic databases if other databases are unlikely to provide all relevant evidence

STANDARD 3.2
Take action to address potentially biased reporting of research results

3.2.1 Search grey literature databases, clinical trial registries, and other sources of unpublished information about studies

3.2.2 Invite researchers to clarify information about study eligibility, study characteristics, and risk of bias

3.2.3 Invite all study sponsors and researchers to submit unpublished data, including unreported outcomes, for possible inclusion in the systematic review

3.2.4 Handsearch selected journals and conference abstracts

3.2.5 Conduct a web search

3.2.6 Search for studies reported in languages other than English if appropriate

STANDARD 3.3
Screen and select studies

3.3.1 Include or exclude studies based on the protocol's prespecified criteria

3.3.2 Use observational studies in addition to randomized clinical trials to evaluate harms of interventions

3.3.3 Use two or more members of the review team, working independently, to screen and select studies

3.3.4 Train screeners using written documentation; test and retest screeners to improve accuracy and consistency

3.3.5 Use one of two strategies to select studies: (1) read all full-text articles identified in the search or (2) screen titles and abstracts of all articles and then read the full text of articles identified in initial screening

3.3.6 Taking account of the risk of bias, consider using observational studies to address gaps in the evidence from randomized clinical trials on the benefits of interventions

STANDARD 3.4

Document the search

3.4.1 Provide a line-by-line description of the search strategy, including the date of every search for each database, web browser, etc.

3.4.2 Document the disposition of each report identified including reasons for their exclusion if appropriate

STANDARD 3.5

Manage data collection

3.5.1 At a minimum, use two or more researchers, working independently, to extract quantitative and other critical data from each study. For other types of data, one individual could extract the data while the second individual independently checks for accuracy and completeness. Establish a fair procedure for resolving discrepancies—do not simply give final decision-making power to the senior reviewer

3.5.2 Link publications from the same study to avoid including data from the same study more than once

3.5.3 Use standard data extraction forms developed for the specific systematic review

3.5.4 Pilot-test the data extraction forms and process

STANDARD 3.6

Critically appraise each study

3.6.1 Systematically assess the risk of bias, using predefined criteria

3.6.2 Assess the relevance of the study's populations, interventions, and outcome measures

3.6.3 Assess the fidelity of the implementation of interventions

Standards for Synthesizing the Body of Evidence

NOTE: The order of the standards does not indicate the sequence in which they are carried out.

STANDARD 4.1

Use a prespecified method to evaluate the body of evidence

4.1.1 For each outcome, systematically assess the following characteristics of the body of evidence:
  · Risk of bias
  · Consistency
  · Precision
  · Directness
  · Reporting bias

4.1.2 For bodies of evidence that include observational research, also systematically assess the following characteristics for each outcome:
  · Dose-response association
  · Plausible confounding that would change the observed effect
  · Strength of association

4.1.3 For each outcome specified in the protocol, use consistent language to characterize the level of confidence in the estimates of the effect of an intervention

STANDARD 4.2

Conduct a qualitative synthesis

4.2.1 Describe the clinical and methodological characteristics of the included studies, including their size, inclusion or exclusion of important subgroups, timeliness, and other relevant factors

4.2.2 Describe the strengths and limitations of individual studies and patterns across studies

4.2.3 Describe, in plain terms, how flaws in the design or execution of the study (or groups of studies) could bias the results, explaining the reasoning behind these judgments

4.2.4 Describe the relationships between the characteristics of the individual studies and their reported findings and patterns across studies

4.2.5 Discuss the relevance of individual studies to the populations, comparisons, cointerventions, settings, and outcomes or measures of interest

STANDARD 4.3

Decide if, in addition to a qualitative analysis, the systematic review will include a quantitative analysis (meta-analysis)

4.3.1 Explain why a pooled estimate might be useful to decision makers

STANDARD 4.4

If conducting a meta-analysis, then do the following:

4.4.1 Use expert methodologists to develop, execute, and peer review the meta-analyses

4.4.2 Address the heterogeneity among study effects

4.4.3 Accompany all estimates with measures of statistical uncertainty

4.4.4 Assess the sensitivity of conclusions to changes in the protocol, assumptions, and study selection (sensitivity analysis)

Standards for Reporting Systematic Reviews

STANDARD 5.1
Prepare final report using a structured format

5.1.1 Include a report title

5.1.2 Include an abstract

5.1.3 Include an executive summary

5.1.4 Include a summary written for the lay public

5.1.5 Include an introduction (rationale and objectives)

5.1.6 Include a methods section. Describe the following:
- Research protocol
- Eligibility criteria (criteria for including and excluding studies in the systematic review)
- Analytic framework and key questions
- Databases and other information sources used to identify relevant studies
- Search strategy
- Study selection process
- Data extraction process
- Methods for handling missing information
- Information to be extracted from included studies
- Methods to appraise the quality of individual studies
- Summary measures of effect size (e.g., risk ratio, difference in means)
- Rationale for pooling (or not pooling) results of included studies
- Methods of synthesizing the evidence (qualitative and meta-analysis)
- Additional analyses, if done, indicating which were prespecified

5.1.7 Include a results section. Organize the presentation of results around key questions. Describe the following (repeat for each key question):
- Study selection process
- List of excluded studies and reasons for their exclusion
- Appraisal of individual studies' quality
- Qualitative synthesis
- Meta-analysis of results, if performed (explain rationale for doing one)
- Additional analyses, if done, indicating which were prespecified
- Tables and figures

5.1.8 Include a discussion section. Include the following:
- Summary of the evidence
- Strengths and limitations of the systematic review
- Conclusions for each key question
- Gaps in evidence
- Future research needs

5.1.9 Include a section describing funding sources and COI

STANDARD 5.2
Peer review the draft report

5.2.1 Use a third party to manage the peer review process

5.2.2 Provide a public comment period for the report and publicly report on disposition of comments

STANDARD 5.3
Publish the final report in a manner that ensures free public access

INSTITUTE OF MEDICINE
OF THE NATIONAL ACADEMIES

Advising the nation • Improving health

500 Fifth Street, NW
Washington, DC 20001
TEL 202.334.2352
FAX 202.334.1412

www.iom.edu

The Institute of Medicine serves as adviser to the nation to improve health.
Established in 1970 under the charter of the National Academy of Sciences, the Institute of Medicine provides independent, objective, evidence-based advice to policy makers, health professionals, the private sector, and the public.

Index

About the Author

Librarian Emerita **Terry Ann Jankowski**, MLS, AHIP, FMLA, has over 40 years of experience as an expert searcher. She participated in the development of database searching from the slow dial-up era to today's high-speed Wi-Fi access on the web.

Throughout her career, Ms. Jankowski has focused on database searching, reference services, user education, and user services. She has authored several publications and presentations on these topics. She started her career at the University of Southern California Norris Medical Library as a reference librarian. At the University of Washington Health Sciences Library, she began as a reference librarian and progressed through coordinating the online search service to managing the education program and finished as assistant director for user experience. An active volunteer in the Medical Library Association, she has served on a number of committees, editorial boards, and task forces, usually in the searching or professional development arenas. Ms. Jankowski continues to revise and teach her course on expert searching.